To my: (Richard

always (Rosie

THE THOUGHT OF YOU

The Art of Being Alive!

Rosie Wolf Williams

TABLE OF CONTENTS

INTRODUCTION

Life can be confusing.

You might wonder why you are here on this earth, in this lifetime. Is there a purpose beyond working and paying bills? Are you here to bring about world peace, or to invent a new product? Are you here to help someone else along in their journey to enlightenment? Or are you playing a lead role in a grand play that only you can write?

You might be here to do all those things. It's completely up to you.

Have you ever felt regret? Your regrets may begin with "I didn't."

I didn't take that dream vacation.

I didn't say I love you enough.

I didn't make a difference in the lives of others.

You forget which way you wanted to go, or what you wanted to do. Like when you walk into a room to get something and immediately forget why you went in there. We can all relate, right?

In 2009, I was at a hospital in Philadelphia – I had been diagnosed with cancer, and I was scheduled for surgery the next day. I met a man named David, who was scheduled for surgery at the same time. He was tall, dark, and quiet. My complete opposite. We liked each other. David asked if we could hang out that night.

David sat in the lobby chair, his long legs stretched out, a hospital-sized water bottle balanced on his knee. He told me about his children and his failed marriage, his work in Pittsburgh, his sweet little dog that he had just sent off to a friend. He talked about his dream to be a pilot – a passion that he abandoned early on in his life.

He told me about his cancer diagnosis. He said, "I don't think I'm going to wake up from tomorrow's surgery."

He seemed to relax after saying it aloud. "Are you okay with that?" I asked him.

"I am," he answered. After a long pause, he said, "I do have one regret... I regret that over the years I forgot why I was here."

When we come into this life to have this big adventure, it's as if we walk into another room. We instantly forget why we came here. Sometimes we spend our entire lives trying to remember what it was that we were supposed to do. But we can't go back to help us remember.

David had come to the end of his time here, and he felt he should have done more, experienced more, played more. He had stopped having fun. He had forgotten the true meaning of life itself.

He forgot why he was here.

Life should not be about having regrets. The great poet Omar Khayyam said, "Be happy for this moment. This moment is your life."

Why are you here?

Long ago, before you were simply you in this body, you played in the depths of awareness and unlimited possibility as part of a larger connected base. Along the way, you dipped your toes into the sea of experience, and began to explore newly created worlds in limited form. By exploring as a formed being, you begin to understand how unlimited you once were. To expand your knowledge, you often must compress your world. You forget where you came from. You forget what is really important, what is temporary, and what is ever-expanding. You forget who you are at your core.

You were created by you, by part of something bigger than what can fit into your body, to do something spectacular. You are part of something more expansive than you can imagine, and you were a part of the plan that included you and everyone else around you. Your ability to create and manifest the world you live in has no end, and you still have the power to tap into the larger awareness, The Knowing, for assistance.

You came into being by choice, and you continue to choose your way through life now.

What will you choose? You have the backing of all of us, because we all arrived in the same way – a part of something bigger and more powerful than ourselves. We all sprang from a single thought: to be alive.

And here you are – I've been waiting for you! You and I are on this journey together, and your thoughts will determine which path you take.

Your life is not determined by your birth – your circumstances are simply where you chose to begin this journey, and you arrived with a pre-determined set of events. You can resign yourself to existing within those pre-determined boundaries, or you can find a way out of that situation and discover new ways of thinking, of creating, or of being. Buddhism often speaks of life as a continuous occurrence of birth and death. Your journey does not have an end, because all things are connected. All things are a part of the greater awareness, and will return again and again in a new or different form.

You, my friend, are a seeker of truth. You are thought, and thought is infinite.

This book will help you to understand your power as a finite being within an infinite awareness. The ideas that I offer are simply discoveries I have made on my own journey in this lifetime, and perhaps collected on journeys of the past. Every event has been determined by my own thoughts or the thoughts of others, and I alone had the power to react to them and change my direction. In some cases, I took my sweet time figuring out what was best. In others, I quickly recalled past events and made more positive decisions. But all of them helped me learn and grow.

They helped me remember.

Understand how you came about, and how you can again "remember" that you have the power to make your life matter. The power you have is there whether you know it or not – whether you choose the way it is used or not. Your thoughts manifest your world, and you can allow your thoughts to run wild with negativity or you can create a more positive outcome by dumping worry or other negative thoughts and living each moment with purpose. You can experience and love more just by being alive.

Not every word in this book will resonate with you. That's okay. You still hold the oar of free will and choice, and only you can navigate your life. But if

one passage in this book makes you stop and pon-
der the possibilities of a more satisfying, more purposeful life, then run with it. Make it your own. You
are here because of my thoughts and of your own
– now read on and discover how amazing you are.

I am so grateful we found each other.

CHAPTER 1: THE THOUGHT OF YOU

What are you thinking? Right now? By the time you read the question, you may have thought of several things. These thoughts can be fleeting or concrete. You might think in words, symbols, or pictures. Thinking is the core of all mental processes and the heart of reality.

If I ask you to think of a pink butterfly, what do you see in your mind? Just that – a pink butterfly. Your thought creates a vision that you can recognize as the form of the thought. But your vision of that butterfly is unique to you. You may have thought of a pink butterfly with darker spots on its wings. Or it may have been sitting on your hand or fluttering about. You created the butterfly in your mind, and no one else knows exactly how it looks.

But your thoughts can create more than a simple vision of a pink butterfly. An inventor thinks of a solution to a problem and turns that thought into a product. One person can look at an event and think it's a disaster, and another is able to think that it's an opportunity. And they are both right. Their thoughts are personal, and they create their outlook on the world.

Describing thought is difficult because it has no form and takes on all forms, is in all things, cannot be destroyed, and can create beyond measure. Words can only offer a partial description of the masterpiece of a thought. But let's try.

●   ●   ●

Everything you see and everything that exists around you is comprised of something beyond the physical. If you look at the human body, you would probably agree that you are a big cooperative group of cells. But if you go beyond the cell, what do you have?

Well, not much – at least that you can spy with your little eye.

Scientists say that most of the cells in your body regenerate every 7 to 15 years. But not everything is actually thrown away. Much of the old cell is reused, recycled, restructured – using ancient particles that have existed for millions of years. Some of these materials once existed in stars, and some were created in the explosion of stars.

If you could travel deep inside one of your cells and break it down even further, you would eventually discover that cells are made up of something called quarks, and they're held together with gluons. But if you try to pull those quarks apart with a lot of energy, more quarks appear as if by magic, creating a "quark soup."

Abracadabra – there you are, you beautiful human being, you.

Your body's mass is made of energy and stardust. And even the stardust was once pure energy.

Now, don't you feel sparkly?

It gets even more complex.

●   ●   ●

You, my friend, began from a grander thought that used vibrating energy and leftover stardust to blast you into form.

Let's assume you agree with the theory that all

physical things in our world – every rock, every animal, mountain, or grain of sand – has the same base components, and they are all vibrating on some level to hold a form or emit a sound or perform an action. The water, the air, and the planets in our universe all hold energy that is consistent with the energy within ourselves. We are all the same – one at the very core. The ocean is the drop of water, and the drop of water is the ocean.

Your thoughts can be singular, within you, or they can share a larger community. You can create or determine a thought with or without outside help. Your thoughts can come from within your own personal soup, or you can perceive and form a thought by grabbing energy from other sources – which, in the grand scheme of things, is also you.

Metaphysical thinking and intuition is just barely hiding behind physics. As scientists dig deeper, more theories arise that might make you scratch your head and wonder if it is all too complicated to even describe. Where does your knowledge come from, and where does wisdom begin?

● ● ●

Descartes said, "I think, therefore I am." But thought guru Deepak Chopra explains that he would modify that statement.

"We have individual minds, of course, and at the same time we participate in a collective mind." Chopra says, "I prefer to say, 'I am, therefore I think.' Existence comes first. Or to be more precise, if consciousness is at the very heart of creation, we cannot separate it from existence."

So if you put a ladle full of soup into a bowl, the soup does not become something different, nor does the pot of soup cease to exist. Chopra's explanation of consciousness, or existence, is the soup from which you came.

You are made from this purest form of consciousness. Let's call it The Knowing. We will talk more about that later. The Knowing allows you to understand the connectedness of everything while still embracing your own individuality. To hold form in this way is to have free will, choice, and to experience love in special ways. Being human and individual is an adventure you take as part of that larger whole – to experience, to make mistakes, to vibrate in a particular universe that holds you in with skin and bones, quarks and gluons, stardust and energy. You vibrate at a unique level. Through your thoughts, you can choose to change the vibration of your own mind and body at will. When you do so, the vibration around you changes to meet your own – like water seeks level. Like attracts like. It is the universal law of attraction.

● ● ●

You are thought in form. You think. You do it on a daily basis, whether you try to think or not. It just happens. You are plugged into an energetic force that offers you access to continuous thought and gives you the ability to think – just like you plug in your clock or your computer to receive energy. But every thought is being matched by a vibration inside and outside your physical body, and that vibration begins to form that thought into reality.

Thought is, in my opinion, inclusive of and beyond the workings of the physical brain. It is at the core of all that is, all that you see – and all that you don't see – with your physical capabilities. The problem is that its description won't fit into a soup bowl or a specific socially acceptable way of thinking. It is the soup bowl. It is also the soup, and the pot, and the air around the pot.

It is truly whatever you would like it to be. Which means that you are not wrong or right, and neither is the guy who decides to think of it as something different from your own vision. It is an all-encompassing, all-inclusive energy that never ends and never begins. Just embrace each other, because you are them, and they are you. You can send your thoughts out to The Knowing, and someone else could direct theirs to God, to Allah, to the Universe, or to the Man on the Mountain – and all those thoughts will end up in a pile in the same mailbox, waiting for their turn to become reality.

And here's the cool thing about thought and The Knowing. Whether you believe it or not, it still works.

You can close your eyes and ask yourself what you imagine as thought. You might see turtles and astronauts and the color red. You might close your eyes and ask yourself the same question in another hour, and you might see visions of yellow school busses, burnt toast, and flugelhorns. Thought can take on any form at any time. Whatever you focus on in your conscious and unconscious mind, the vibration in The Knowing matches it.

● ● ●

The idea of an infinite connection and consciousness does not exclude religions or souls, nor does it expect certain rituals or traditions in order to create. You are capable of using whatever ritual or symbol or sign or language you would like to unlock your infinite potential.

You may follow the religion and tradition of your parents, peers, or ancestors. You might worship a god or gods, a symbol or sign. You may memorize a psalm or a chant. It's okay that you do that. Do you have peace? Do you offer peace? Choose a way that allows you to transcend the teachings of any religion or science, allowing awareness without blocking or excluding.

There is no randomness in your life. There is meaning. Everything matters, and nothing matters. It is infinite in form, function, substance, emotion, and awareness. Even by describing it in that way, you are limiting it to a mere speck of its true possibility. The power of thought is unlimited, and you are capable of creating so much more than you ever thought possible.

What is thought?

Thought is you.

PRACTICE

Let's practice forming a teeny tiny reality from thought:

Close your eyes. Think of your favorite color. Your thought probably formed a word in your mind or a little swatch of the color you thought of. So let's take it to a higher level. Think of something that has that color. If you picked blue, you might think of a blueberry, a blue van, or a blue bird. Form the thought in your mind, and then tell yourself you know and believe that you will manifest a blue bird or blue car in the next 12 or 24 hours. It will become a reality for you. Think deeply about this manifestation for at least 30 seconds. Then open your eyes, knowing in your heart that you will see the results of your thoughts.

Sometimes our manifestations don't appear in exactly the same form that we anticipate. An imagined elephant may appear as a part of a fabric print or a picture on a postcard. A red car might manifest as a showcased prize in a casino, or it might pull up as you are waiting for a taxi in front of your hotel.

Try this exercise several times. Try it until you believe it. Because it will make bigger things become more believable.

SUMMARY

- Our physical body is constantly regenerating.
- Cells are made up of quarks and gluons, that multiply and create a larger "soup" of cells.
- We are all the same at our core.
- You are able to form a thought within you or from out side sources.
- You are made from the purest form of consciousness.

CHAPTER 2: YOU ARE NOT ALONE

When I was a little girl, I woke up in the middle of the night, and I saw a large object hovering over the steeple of a nearby church. I watched it without fear for some time before I fell back to sleep. The next morning, I told my parents about it. I described the lights and the way the object seemed to float over the cemetery at the side of the church building. I was matter-of-fact, accepting that it was there – but wanting to know more.

You might think that my father would say that I was imagining things or that I was dreaming. Instead, he acknowledged that I may have seen a UFO. I don't remember his exact explanation, but I do remember his pure trust and belief in what I saw. He said something like "Shorty, we don't know it all. It's a great big space out there, and it never ends." He told me that we humans would have to have pretty enormous egos to think that we are the only ones here in the Universe.

● ● ●

Dad allowed me to think about possibility – to

create my own beliefs about that hovering light, and wonder what more there was out in that great darkness. He claimed that our planet is simply a tiny speck in an infinite and undefined space.

I am interested in and open to the possibility of everything – other worlds, creation, unidentified life forms, Bigfoot, spirits, angels, crystals, magic – you name it. I won't say it can't be true. I say, why not? If thought is indeed inclusive of and beyond the workings of the physical brain, then wouldn't anything be possible?

You have the power to believe what you want to believe. You may have decided that life is only possible on your own planet Earth. That there is no possible way that other living beings exist on other planets or in different forms other than your own. Or you might think that if there is life out there, it has only evolved to form a one-celled organism, and it could not be intelligent enough to travel to your planet or attempt to communicate with you.

Humans once believed the world was flat (and some still do), that Earth was at the center of the universe, and that the sun revolved around the

Earth. And then popular opinion changed. Why not, then, believe that once your thoughts turn to infinite possibility, that your world and your reality also gets larger?

●   ●   ●

The thoughts of a higher consciousness, The Knowing, also plays a part in your life. There is an origin of thought that conjures up everything that has happened before you and before your ancestors and their ancestors. Something created your world and everything beyond. The laws of time and space, the law of gravity, the law of attraction, and all the laws that play into the world as you know it were blasted into being in some way. You are connected to The Knowing and can receive or offer thought as a part of a collective consciousness that extends beyond your own reality. There is also a template of life for you as an individual. Perhaps a game plan that you chose before you started your journey in your current form.

Scientists debate a theory called "objective reality." The term essentially means that you and other human beings co-create the world you see. You say it is real because you agree to that idea. You agreed that this would be the concept, and you constructed it accordingly. It is man-made. But reality is created in your mind, through your thoughts, so you're never actually sure of what you are seeing, nor does the person next to you see the same picture.

The boundaries set up by social or community thought work only in the physical world. For instance, a road or a wall or a building is the result of more than one thought in its creation. A law or perceived social behavior or custom is also the thought of many. You can of course break a law. Laws are the result of many physical beings agreeing with what should be done at the moment.

But those laws are also not permanent. They change or disappear.

●   ●   ●

Women's and civil rights have been enacted after some brave individuals refused to allow an imbalance of rights. Why believe that because you think you cannot break down barriers now, that you cannot do so by changing the way you think about your potential? A simple statement like "Mr. Gor-bachev, tear down that wall," inspired hundreds of people to do just that, piece by piece, until a structure that divided a city and its inhabitants was simply a memory.

Even as a young girl, I had a basic understand-ing of how thought somehow becomes reality, how dreams come true. When I became an adult, I would mention something to that effect in conversation, and people would say to me, oh, you must have read the works of Dr. Wayne Dyer, or Eckhart Tolle, or other spiritualists. At the time, I hadn't read the books, and I thought, well, maybe I need to read them. The more I read, the more I realized that I wasn't alone in my theories. It was exciting for me to know that what I felt from the moment I could remember things was actually a deeper truth. I had, in fact, developed my own truth from the one truth.

"We all tap in, in a different way, the beautiful paradox of being human," says Dianne Collins, au-thor of *Do You QuantumThink?: New Thinking That Will Rock Your World.* "We're universally the same and individually unique. It's part of the old world-view conditioning that we want to compare, rather than actually take something in as a new thought."

Your mind is powerful. More powerful than you can even imagine. You create your reality through thought, which becomes belief, action, or even inaction.

* * *

Perhaps before you took on your current form as dancing stardust, you originally created a setting of poverty or privilege, of tragedy or temperance, giving you a starting point for your adventure. But that setting is not your result – it is your beginning. You can choose to change the terrain of your life journey, by considering other options and creating a different reality. When you decided to experience a linear existence, you also gave yourself free will and choice. You discover your own truths.

So you follow your truth. But there are many sides to what you would call truth, and depending on which side you view, the truth looks a bit different. The famous Schrödinger's Cat experiment might illustrate that. Schrödinger argues that the theory called the Copenhagen interpretation implies that a cat in a box is both dead and alive until the cat is observed when the box is eventually opened. The cat remains in superposition – and is neither dead nor alive – until someone is there to perceive it. Schrödinger said the idea is ridiculous.

However, if we return to the idea in Chapter 1 – that our bodies are constantly regenerating and that living things are made up of not only matter but energy – you could honestly say that the cat is both dead and alive at that moment. The cells may die, but the energy does not. Is the cat dead or alive? The truth is in the mind of the person who answers. If a person views the cat as dead inside the box, the cat is dead. If he sees that cat as alive, he is alive.

Now most likely, Schrödinger was simply trying to debunk the Copenhagen interpretation, because he thought it was ridiculous. I'm sure he was not trying to forever attach his name to a cat in a box. He might not have even owned a cat. But by creating the "what if" of the cat in the box, that cat has become alive through the experiment itself.

●   ●   ●

You could take that one step further. If you believe the cat in the box is dead, you might walk away dejected, not in any hurry to open that box because you already know the cat is beyond help. But if you believe the cat is alive, you rush to open the box to allow the cat to break free and breathe. You take immediate action to make sure the cat is in fact alive and will continue to live. You may in fact save the cat's life by opening the box! The cat is alive while he experiences an energy/matter existence. And once he is not, he is pure energy, ready to reform into something else.

If you say, "I'm a failure. Nothing ever goes right for me. If something bad can happen, it will," you are probably right in that moment. You think and support the belief that you are a failure. So, you act like a failure, which creates situations that re-inforce your belief of failure. Therefore, you must be a failure, right? It is a never-ending circle of self battering.

Someone might say to you, "No! You are not a failure!" You consider their perspective, and you might change your own thoughts. You can redis-cover your power and choose more productive and positive thoughts that will change your future. Your new thoughts can stop the drought of negativity by allowing a trickle of optimism to quench your thirst. You could be the guy who rushes to open the box to let the cat out and show everyone that there is more to your world than that stinky old box.

● ● ●

You can inspire others to do the same. This is especially important with children when they are still working on self-esteem, morals, ethics, and compassion. Your words of encouragement can have a tremendous effect on their growth and potential.

Once you draw a conclusion and create a recurring thought that you are a failure or a success, you subconsciously look for the evidence that reinforces your belief. You might also dismiss any evidence that would contradict your belief. If you believe you are a failure, you will list all your mistakes and poor decisions as proof. You will point out your inability to know enough or your lack of money or other external reasons for failing. And if you do succeed at anything, you might call it "dumb luck" or say that you will somehow find a way to "mess it all up." Others may give you support in this way as well, saying "Wow, what got into you?" or "You'll figure out how to sabotage yourself," or "This won't last."

But all is not lost – just as easily as you can create your belief of failure, you can create a vision of success. A positive outlook can lead to positive outcomes.

Your outlook leads to your outcome.

●   ●   ●

Positive thoughts are the beginning of a change in the vibration, of the sparks that fly in your brain, in those little puffs of energy that might be thought. You can alter your perception and change your life.

Your mind isn't limited to the boundaries of the world around you. It is a part of the greater mind, The Knowing, and is a part of the all-encompassing consciousness. It transcends the world as you see it. As a result, the ideas that party in your brain also have contact with the brains of other beings and the rest of that thought soup. Thoughts can scatter far and wide, take form, and turn up in the oddest of places.

Marconi and Tesla both had similar thoughts at around the same time in the 1890s. But they chose to take action in different ways. Both men were working on the creation of the radio, and Tesla received more of the early patents for the technology. Marconi is credited with developing the first working system of radio communication.

But electromagnetic radiation was made years earlier by German scientist Heinrich Hertz, who was able to both transmit and receive radio waves in his lab. He just didn't think of how to use it in a practical way.

Sometimes thoughts are not sparked by watching or hearing something. You may have thought of someone you hadn't heard from in a long while, only to have someone else mention that person the very same day. Or the person in question calls out of the blue, saying they couldn't stop thinking about you. Siblings often think of the same things at the same time, regardless of the physical distance between them.

●   ●   ●

This ability to share thoughts does not end with friends or relatives. In 2014, neuroscientist Carlos Grau of the University of Barcelona and his colleagues used transcranial stimulators to transmit the thoughts of subjects in India over the internet to subjects in France.

The subjects in India generated an EEG signal that was to represent either a one or a zero by using a biofeedback monitor. To generate a one or a zero, the subjects imagined moving a hand or a foot. The ones and zeros were then emailed from India to France and routed to one of two TMS devices mounted on subjects' scalps.

The experiment was sort of a Morse Code from one subject to another through the use of thought. Error rates were low enough for the experiment to be considered as a success – subjects were able to send simple thoughts to another person in another country.

You are thinking messages to others right now, however it is not considered scientific evidence and is often labeled hokey or woo-woo.

A writing colleague and I have often joked about this: how we will brainstorm ideas and come up with a great story subject, only to open a magazine a few months later to discover someone else had written an article on the same subject. Have we communicated our idea to the writer or has her focus on her article been transmitted to us?

"A nonlocal mind doesn't have a physical existence in the same way as dense or physical matter, and so it can go anywhere," says Dianne Collins. "It doesn't actually 'travel'—our minds simply *connect*. With intuition you can hook into any intelligence anywhere, or connect to another person across the globe."

●　●　●

Thought impacts your life at base level, but in so many ways. You think about your daily schedules and actions. Your community thinks up ordinances and bylaws. Your country comes up with ideas and thoughts on how to preserve and protect. Your world accepts a social order. And beyond that, thought has created the space/time/reality you live in. The Universe is ever-expanding. You were thought into existence, and you can create our own world by thinking.

You are thought.

So why are some of your thoughts changeable and others not changeable?

Remember, you made a few agreements before becoming the form that is currently you. Your form, your existence, gives you limits through a larger collective thought, but also allows free will and choice through your own thoughts. By changing your thoughts to improve or impair your reality, you affect the thoughts of others, which affects the thoughts of others, and so on. Your vibration of thought ripples out to change the texture and terrain of your shared reality. Like attracts like – when your vibration shifts, the vibration around you shifts, too.

Have you ever heard the statement, "When Mama's not happy, nobody's happy?" Mama is a key player in a family, and her mood of the moment vibrates and ripples out to others in the household. Have you walked into a room after two people have been arguing, and the air is so thick and heavy you feel like you could cut it with a knife? The vibration of the argument between the two people has charged the room and attracted a like vibration. I would imagine that you couldn't wait to get out of that room – or you joined in the fray.

But if you experience a baby's pure laughter, cuddle up to a favorite person, or watch a funny movie, you can feel the positive energy. It uplifts your spirit and makes you smile. It was all originally created by thought.

As a tiny speck living on a tiny speck in an infinite and undefined space, you can as an individual or as part of a community create a burst of change. Thoughts turn into things, ideas take on form, and fiction can easily become fact. The greatest flow of change and evolution is beyond your physical eye and in the folds and creases of The Knowing.

The hovering object I saw that night so long ago may have held a being that thought about me, or someone like me, who might reach out across the divide without fear of the unknown – and there I was.

Pick up your cell phone and call someone – they've already thought you would.

PRACTICE

Take a few moments to focus on someone you haven't heard from in a while. Imagine this person thinking of you, picking up the phone, or typing an email to you. Imagine yourself receiving this communication and smiling because you are so happy to connect with this person again. Then, wait to see if you manifest a phone call or email.

SUMMARY

- We are tiny specks in an infinite and undefined space.
- Reality is created in our minds, through our thoughts, and the person next to you does not see the same picture.
- A law or perceived social behavior or custom is also the thought of many.
- We are given free will and choice to discover our own truths.
- Your outlook leads to your outcome.
- Like attracts like – when our vibration shifts, the vibration around us shifts, too.

CHAPTER 3: HOLD ON, LET GO

My father used to repeat an old folk saying when I was young, impulsive, and impatient. He said, "Don't push the river. Just paddle your own canoe." That saying stayed with me over the years, and became more meaningful as I began to navigate my own life as an adult. To try to push the river was to become impatient with the natural flow of things, to try to make time satisfy my needs, to make slow-moving currents faster or white-water events slow down. But I could paddle my own canoe – making decisions that were best for me, taking action when needed, and gathering the things that made the most sense for my personal journey.

●   ●   ●

You have come into your current existence with a predetermined curriculum, one that can be modified or even changed. As part of The Knowing, you have set up boundaries for yourself, including social limits and conditions of the world in which you live.

Those pre-determined boundaries include the place of your birth. You arrive in a certain form, and your body is your only personal vehicle for the entire ride. You have blue eyes or brown eyes, you wear a certain size shoe, you have physical disabilities and strengths. You are set up for an amazing time here as a living, breathing human.

You may encounter certain conditions along the way that are less than comfortable or desirable, but it might all be part of your personal journey. That journey is linear, but varies according to many factors that occur. You could say the existence you have taken on is a river that sprouts from a larger undefinable source, and at its end, it spills back into that larger source.

●　●　●

How do you know what to allow, and what to intend?

Let's imagine for a moment that your life is in fact a river that flows through and from The Knowing.

This river has rough white rapids; smooth, re-flective pools; and soft-flowing ripples. It moves in one direction. It erodes hard, rocky shores and soft earth forms. It overflows banks and creates pools. It feeds and nourishes, but it can also destroy.

Now, take a look back to the moments before you became you. There you are, still sparkling and not yet in form ready to become alive. You stand at the edge of the river, knowing that the river is a vision of your pre-determined set of circumstances. This is the setting of your new adventure, and certain events or people you meet along the way will also play a part in your travels. You have chosen an experience, parents, a location, and perhaps even events and circumstances to make the journey exciting.

Wow! A new adventure – one that will allow you to expand and experience the gifts that come along with taking form.

●　●　●

Now what?

Maybe you decide to jump in and swim the first part of your journey, because you want a true challenge. You dive in, and dog paddle or breaststroke the entire way. Your priority is simply to not drown. You keep your head above water in the rough rapids, and you might turn over on your back and float happily during the good times.

Or you choose a vessel – let's call it a canoe – to use to travel your life river. The canoe you choose is your base emotion, the vibration you arrive with when you are born. You could choose a canoe of anger or happiness or any other core emotion.

You can float along the river, simply following the current and allowing the canoe to float freely at times, lazily drifting along in the center of the river, enjoying the view. The river's current could carry the canoe closer to the shallow banks, scrape against the rocks, or be punctured by a log. You are happy when the water is calm, but you feel out of control and threatened when your canoe moves into rougher currents.

But your canoe comes with paddles that allow you to navigate the river – free will and choice. The paddles give you more control over your safety and well-being. They allow you to make detours, to keep the canoe upright during rough water, to move close to an interest, to take a risk, or to avoid danger.

* * *

At any point in your travels on the river, you can detour to a riverbank and switch one canoe for another. You may know some people who have lived the first part of their journey through anger or resentment. Then through some epiphany or event, they have suddenly discovered happiness, or compassion. You always have control over the switch.

As you travel, you see opportunities float by like pieces of driftwood, and you can pick them up and put them in your canoe. Relationships, material objects, jobs and careers – some appear under your fingertips, but others pop up just beyond your reach. You might have to put some effort into grabbing the ones that seem to be perfect for your needs. Some rush by as if they are caught in a different current, and you have to snatch them out of the water before they disappear around the bend.

You also have the choice to toss something out of your canoe if it turns out to be something different than you imagined. Or you could ignore it altogether, never picking it up, letting it drift away or get caught on the rocks.

●　●　●

Wow, so many opportunities! So much beauty!

You decide to pick up as many pieces of drift-wood as possible, and soon your canoe is filled with so many unnecessary things that it isn't so easy to maneuver. It's weighted down and is so close to the water's surface that you are in danger of sinking. You are cramped and have no space to use your paddles of free will and choice, so you simply poke at those sharp rocks or overhanging branches in the hopes that you can keep them from harming you. You see an amazing opportunity float within reach, but you are unable to find room for it.

Then the river gets rougher.

The water starts lapping over the top of your ca-noe and you bare-knuckle the whole ride, rolling up in a ball at the bottom of your canoe and not daring to look out at that scary river. You look at the pad-dles but shout, "I can't!" and you hear the biggest and knobbiest of those driftwood pieces knocking against the sides. You clutch the things that you picked out of the water along the way and hide behind them. You don't reach out. You don't take a chance. You close your eyes, because if you look, there might be a giant, slimy river monster staring at you, dripping with saliva, ready to chomp on your bones. You are afraid of the whole trip along the river, and you can't wait for it to end.

Have you forgotten that you have power to change the scene?

You have control over your thoughts, but you also must remember to allow and trust the outside forces.

You can control your thoughts and beliefs by consciously changing them. Once you have changed the thought, and made efforts to take a course (even a slightly different one), The Knowing takes hold of that thought and vibrates to match it. It allows like energy to appear and begin to revolve in your space, offering opportunity and circumstances that help that intent become a reality.

That slimy monster suddenly dissolves into a million fragrant water lilies.

The river itself is predetermined, but you have the complete power to change your circumstances.

You are in control of your journey!

* * *

The phrase "the pursuit of happiness" is misleading. It leads you to believe that happiness is an elusive thing that floats just ahead. You would never consider allowing the canoe to drift ahead of you while you desperately breaststroke behind it, trying to catch it. You don't have to pursue anything.

You already have it.

Happiness is what you ride in. Without it the journey is doable - but so much more difficult. If you want that challenge of swimming just out of reach of the canoe, you have the power to make that choice as well. Or you can make it to the end of the river, realizing that the happiness you expected to find is still sitting at the starting point, empty and meaningless.

Jump in that canoe right now. Be happy. Then

push off with confidence.

It's never too late to change your journey. Once you decide you want to continue in happiness instead of pursuing it, you will be presented with it. The Knowing will match the desire with the outcome.

● ● ●

What happens if you capsize, or you decide to jump out?

It happens to the most skilled navigators. We sometimes forget that we own it, and we can reclaim it in the blink of an eye. A traumatic event, a struggle in a relationship, or the loss of a loved one might upset the balance of things, and over you go.

The paddles of free will and choice float free, and they become tools to help you stay afloat. You might swim and make progress, but you really aren't able reach out to collect the driftwood – the opportunities that come along – because you are too busy swimming. One might come so close that you can grab it and hold on for a while, but when the water gets rougher, you have to let go just to survive or let go of those all-important paddles in order to hold on to the opportunity.

Remember how important the canoe is. Swim to a riverbank, catch your breath, dry off a little. Then look around, because when you desire, you will create a new canoe that will serve you well.

●   ●   ●

Because you exist, you must allow some things to be out of your control. Trust that the preconceived river (the one you chose before becoming alive) was going to flow as needed, as fast or as slow as necessary. As part of The Knowing, you have created a game plan with boundaries – your own location, your parents, certain socially accepted realities, events, locations, and other situations that offer you a solid place to start. You let go of the control of the big picture. You are set to play the game.

●   ●   ●

Can you invite another person to share your journey in one canoe, or must you travel alone?

Every person has his or her own canoe. You have

relationships with others when they travel beside you. You hold your own canoes as personal and sacred, so you can continue to be whole in your journey without depending on another to handle the paddles. The right person will take the journey with you, floating alongside and enjoying the view with you. You can share your lovely collection of driftwood with them, but you don't share the canoe.

Just imagine if you decide this person is not cut out to be your traveling companion. Would you feel comfortable tossing him or her overboard? Of course not. By holding your happiness as your own, you could choose to lovingly separate and continue your own journeys in whatever way you choose.

PRACTICE

Just like you created a vision of the pink butterfly, you can create your canoe of happiness in your mind. Is it bright red or rough balsa wood? Does it have symbols or words painted on the sides? It might not even be a canoe. You vision might take the shape of a ship, a raft, or whatever you'd like. Add features to it so you can easily recall the image when necessary.

Look inside and discover the smooth, balanced paddles that wait for you. Envision them and feel them in your hands. They are a perfect length and fit – they have been created just for you!

Then imagine yourself climbing into the canoe and holding the paddles, ready to start your journey. You decide where you go. Your thoughts become your choices, and your choices become your actions. The Knowing matches your strokes of intention with opportunity. As Katharine Hepburn said in her book, *Me: Stories of My Life,* "As one goes through life one learns that if you don't paddle your own canoe, you don't move."

Accept the flow of the journey instead of expecting it to play out in hows and whys. Let the river take your vessel into its current, with you directing it. Breathe. Feel the movement of the river, and allow yourself to enjoy the flow, secure and safe, yet in control. Don't push the river, just allow it to take you along in your journey. Your thoughts will direct you.

Hold on, and let go.

SUMMARY

- Your life is a like river that flows through and from and to The Knowing.
- There might have been a pre-determined set of circumstances to set up this adventure of being alive – but the game is fluid and changeable.
- At the beginning of our journey, we choose a vessel, a canoe, to use to travel the river. That vessel is our base emotion.
- You have a say in how you react to or avoid certain pre-determined socially accepted realities, events, locations, and other situations.
- You have the paddles of free will and choice that give you control over the journey.
- The thoughts and manifestations of others give us opportunities to learn and grow.

CHAPTER 4: WHEN THE THOUGHTS OF OTHERS ARE INVOLVED

You wonder how, if you have such power over your lives, bad things can happen. Trauma, accidents, and other shocking events happen, and you experience loss of some kind along the way.

Remember, you are not alone in your creation. You intend and manifest your situations as an individual, but you also create as part of a community of souls living on earth in the now. If you know this, and you know you have power on your own, you can navigate the community or collective manifestation and events in a meaningful purposeful way. You can use these events whether created by you or as part of the collective, as springboards or steps to a greater, more purposeful place. Whether you manifested through thought (by fear or love) or someone else did, it doesn't matter. What matters is how you direct your thoughts and your actions right now.

●　●　●

How often have we seen people go through horrible situations, and those situations cause them to reassess their lives up to then, and they charge forward with renewed purpose toward a positive goal?

Yes, as you stand here in your living body, things might look tragic and horrible. I personally don't believe in randomness.

In the larger scheme of things, you as part of The Knowing may have pre-planned or caused this event, to complete some greater purpose or satisfy something at a cumulative level, to agree spiritually that you and others are to be at a specific place at a specific time to witness or participate in an event. At that moment, you have free will to choose your actions or reactions. You use thought to experience, to dissolve obstacles, and to expand your knowledge. You have the power to create your future at that moment – to believe that all is lost, or to create a life that is purposeful and focused on happiness.

The body isn't you. You are simply floating in form for the time being. And your mind, inside the body as well as the heart, is the connector to the rest of your consciousness – The Knowing. You not only receive information from The Knowing, but

The Knowing also receives messages from you. What you believe and intend, whether negative or positive, is matched vibrationally, and The Knowing immediately begins to offer you more of what you have focused on.

Your thoughts are vibrations, waves of energy, that interact with you and the world outside of you. Einstein said that matter is made of energy. Matter is what happens when you focus on something – it matters. It matters!

I read something recently, about the wisdom of a little girl. In the story, the girl was asked how she was able to draw so well. She replied that a drawing is a thought with lines around it. To draw, you simply think of something, then you draw lines around the "think."

It is really that simple – what you think about becomes a vision, and with The Knowing's blessing, it becomes reality.

● ● ●

There is an unsubstantiated claim that Michelangelo, when asked how he was able to create such works as David, answered, "I just chip away anything that doesn't look like David." This comment has lightly been attributed to text in an 1858 issue of "The Methodist Quarterly Review." The text goes like this:

"It is the sculptor's power, so often alluded to, of finding the perfect form and features of a goddess, in the shapeless block of marble; and his ability to chip off all extraneous matter, and let the divine excellence stand forth for itself. Thus, in every incident of business, in every accident of life, the poet sees something divine, and carefully scales off all that encumbers that divinity, and permits it to be revealed in all its transcendent loveliness."

This is the same as our lives. We already have everything we need or want inside us, and we only need to chip away the excess or draw lines around the desire to manifest it. It brings it into form.

Whether pre-determined thoughts or the thoughts of others have created a less-than-desired reality, you can focus on the masterpiece inside you instead of the unwanted bits of your progress. When you see your potential, imagine the possibility in this raw and beautiful block of matter, and believe that there is beauty in every chip and crack, it is then that you bring your intentions into form.

There is no randomness in our lives. There is meaning. Everything matters, and nothing matters.

● ● ●

How do you know what is the result of your thought or the result of the thoughts of others?

You don't. And you don't have to know. In fact, you shouldn't even waste time trying to figure it out.

The whole of your reality isn't visible because you are on this linear plane of existence. You can know, however, that thought is infinite in form, function, substance, emotion, and awareness. Even that description is limiting it to a mere speck of its true possibility.

As I mentioned in a previous chapter, my father challenged me to consider a larger picture when I witnessed a UFO as a child. He could have limited my young mind by casting doubt on what I saw that night, perhaps making me wonder if I really saw it at all. Or if I did see it, that I should be afraid of the sight.

While listening to their parents, siblings, and friends, children are like sponges – absorbing information and untruths. When you were a child, you mimicked those you saw as role models or as people in power, and you took on bias and bigotry, acceptance and kindness, or other behaviors as a result. You may have been told "That's just how it is," or "We don't do that," or other statements that create invisible boundaries. The thoughts of others became your own thoughts and manifested into behaviors, which formed your beliefs.

Your thoughts are powerful things. You can think your way into trouble or out of it. And when you change your thoughts, you change your surroundings, your situations, and your world.

⬤ ⬤ ⬤

What do you do if you have taken on behaviors of others, and they no longer serve you?

A behavior is not you. For example, you are not anger. You may behave in an angry way. It is a habit, a learned behavior. Perhaps you learned how to rage and complain while driving by observing how your own parents react to others on the road. And if you have a child in the car – listening to your angry words – you may be offering an example of the same behavior and insensitivity to others, and the child will mimic your actions.

Once you realize that you have the navigating skills to step away, you can choose something different.

"It is just who I am," you might answer.

No - it's not.

It's what you have taken on as a habit for whatever reason. You have the power to change your thoughts, and begin the process of rearranging the vibrations that will become your future.

Think about the people who might have been negative influences in your past or in your current situation. They have come into their lives, using preconceived boundaries, parents, locations, and other situations that set them off on their journey.

Perhaps they signed up to challenge you to become greater. Maybe all the actions they have taken that seem to be obstacles and boundaries are actually helpful to you in some way, to send you on your way to greatness.

PRACTICE

Make a list of the people (past and present) who you feel have hindered you in some way. You may even feel a twinge of hate or deep dislike, repulsion or resentment. Some may have caused you harm. Abuse, disloyalty, or disrespect are very difficult to relive. But now look at these people and situations as tools to lift you to greater heights. They have enabled you to feel compassion and offer kindness to others in similar situations. Find something good, no matter how small or seemingly insignificant, that each person offered you by behaving in that way.

SUMMARY

- Children are like sponges, absorbing information
  and untruths.
  They mimic their role models.
- We limit our power and create invisible boundaries that
  stop us from achieving our goals.
- We can think our way into trouble or out of it. And when
  we change our thoughts, we change our surroundings,
  our situations, and our world.

CHAPTER 5: CHANGING FEAR TO FEAR

I spent much of my young life and into my adult life thinking I could never speak on stage. The idea of standing up in front of other people made me cringe. But as an older adult, I realized that my aversion to public speaking was rooted in a belief that I was not good enough to be seen on stage.

It may have started when I stepped up to deliver a speech in front of my third grade class. I was excited about giving my speech - I was fascinated by pollinators at the time and chose the ant as my subject.

When I began to tell the other kids about ants, most of the other girls in the class made faces or shivered with disgust during the entire presentation. The boys snickered and laughed at the girls' reactions. And I reacted to them, thinking subconsciously that my message was unimportant or laughable. How could I be so stupid? No one wants to hear about ants – I'm the only one in the world who thinks they are interesting! I'll never do this again.

And I didn't, for a long time. I no longer remembered why I had made that choice, but whenever I stood to offer an opinion on something, my face turned red, I started to sweat, and I waited for the snickers and laughter. I had created a reality by believing it was a truth.

*   *   *

Most of my life, I have believed in the power of thought - something that was not yet mainstream. Many times over the years I felt that I should try to fit into the norms of man-made religion or societal regimes. So I felt, deep down inside, that I shouldn't and couldn't talk about the things that were truly at my core, what I believed. I was ashamed to be different and concerned about being ignored or shunned. Ironically, what I thought came true – I didn't share my beliefs, and I was sometimes ignored. My thoughts created my reality.

"Thought is how we represent things, feelings, and events in our mind and the creative agent we use to direct us through life," explains Dr. Ellen Albertson, Board Certified Health & Wellness Coach, Reiki Master, and midlife transformation expert. "Our thoughts can affect our decisions and actions…

when our thoughts are positive we tend to make more positive decisions and take positive actions and have more positive experiences."

One weekend I traveled to Toronto to attend a conference that included top speakers such as Mike Dooley, Dr. Gregg Braden, Dr. Christine Northrup, and others. On the second day of the conference, I watched a speaker take charge of the stage and connect with the audience in a way that inspired me. I knew in that moment that speaking was something I wanted – needed – to do. I had a message to offer to others, and the stage was my next step.

At that moment, I remembered the scene in that classroom of long ago. I understood how my thoughts as a child had turned to belief, and I had turned away from speaking as a result. I realized that my voice did matter, but that I could not control how other beings reacted to it. In that third-grade class, some children did listen and pay attention to my speech on the hard-working little ant. But I had chosen to focus on the louder children, the ones who snickered and laughed, and I took their behavior to heart.

On my way home from the Toronto conference, I made the intention to learn to speak well in front of audiences. Within days of my return, I signed up with a Toastmasters group, so I could practice and develop my skills to speak on stage. I never looked back.

That very first speech about ants taught me a lesson that went way beyond third grade.

Yes, I have felt nervousness over my ability to deliver my message – and that in itself is a message for me to continue my personal work. I had stepped away from my perception of my ability and found that the self-doubt was unfounded. The fear was, in fact, an anxious reflex.

Now when I feel a twinge of nervousness in my stomach, I immediately ask myself, what am I feeling at this moment? Fear and excitement are very close in their symptoms, so I choose to change fear to FEAR – Face Every Anxious Reflex.

• • •

You can begin using FEAR in your everyday life. Let's start with a small example that might make you apprehensive. Perhaps you don't like to make left turns. They make you worry about moving into on-coming traffic, and you imagine the consequences.

Start by making a left turn onto a fairly quiet street. Look both ways for traffic. Pay attention to the feeling in your stomach. If you feel fear, re-label it. Give it a new name. It is now excitement!

How do you feel?

You feel excitement! You are excited about con-quering this issue. You smile, releasing the tension in your face. You shake your hands and let go of the death grip on the steering wheel. Now, look both ways to make sure the road is clear of oncoming traffic, use your turning signals, and off you go.

You did it! You faced your anxious reactions, and you also changed your thoughts and vibrations. You proved to yourself that it wasn't the actual turn that had you scared. It was the belief that you had some-thing to be scared of.

Don't stop there. Next time, try a busier intersec-tion. Use FEAR every step of the way, understand-ing that the twinge you feel can be changed into excitement. Soon, you will make those turns with a smile and wonder why you ever had a problem.

* * *

Using FEAR on a daily basis can open your heart to more possibilities, and you will become excited about opening new doors.

Do you constantly tell yourself, that you're fat or lazy? Do you feel the same apprehension that I did when I had to speak in front of groups?

You think your way to behavior. If you tell yourself that you are fat or lazy, you will continue to bring the same vibration to your reality, confirming that you are fat or lazy. Perhaps fear is compelling you. Is this really who you want to be? Is this something you are proud of – or would you prefer to act in a different way? If so, how do you do it?

You can begin now. Implement FEAR – Face Every Anxious Reflex. You can begin by telling yourself a different story.

Instead of saying, "I would like to lose weight," try saying to yourself, "I weigh an ideal, healthy weight," or "I have so much energy."

Instead of thinking "I feel sick," think "I am healing."

Keep going.

I am graceful. I am considerate of others.

I am fabulous/intelligent/stunning.

Think your way to acting the part. The acting will become the reality.

Believe it! Act like it, and soon you will see a new and improved reality. Tear down your own walls, and let the world in.

PRACTICE

What are you afraid of? Try to go back to the first time it happened. Are you afraid of spiders? Why? Did someone scare you with one when you were a child? Did you watch an adult react to a spider with fear? Break down the reasons for your fear. Reframe it, and take control. Watch a clip of spiders creating webs, or allow yourself to view a picture of a spider until the anxious feeling subsides. Tell yourself a different story about spiders. You may realize, as Mrs. Zuckerman said in the E.B. White classic, "It seems to me we have no ordinary spider."

Make a list of things you want to overcome, and take steps to FEAR by choosing one or two small items on the list. Begin today to change your future.

SUMMARY

- Early events can form life-long behaviors.
- Your behaviors are not you.
- You can face your fear by FEAR – Face Every Anxious Reflex.
- Turn nervousness or panic into excitement.
- Change the outcome by starting small and building up to larger fears.
- Change your statements to yourself – drop negative thoughts and replace with positive statements that reinforce change.

CHAPTER 6: ARE YOU LYING TO YOURSELF?

So facing spiders and making left turns is some-thing you have in your grasp, and you agree that your everyday fears can be conquered with thought. But what about the big events? Did you manifest that car accident or create the illness you have been dealing with? Are you lying to yourself when you think you can make miracles happen?

Although you are an exact replica of the greater consciousness, The Knowing, you are unaware of the grand plan or of the end result of your exis-tence in a linear form. You accepted the challenge to be alive, to discover your power all over again, to become aware as if it were the first time you did so. How much fun would a Monopoly game be if you already knew who would end up with Boardwalk or who would gather the most green houses and red hotels? If you knew the outcome, would you play your best game?

● ● ●

You have taken on a body and entered into this

lifetime with choice and purpose, Some obstacles or events have been mapped out prior to your birth, perhaps by your own spiritual energy. As we discussed earlier, there is free will involved. You can recreate the future of your existence by making conscious choices along the way. For instance, you may have experienced a trauma as a child or suffered a loss of some kind or experienced an illness. You may have felt you were powerless to overcome or avoid that situation. You might be right. It may have been predestined or created through a larger community of thought. You bump into the manifested thoughts of others every day.

However, you are in complete control of your reaction to that trauma or event. And the vibration that you create within your mind – the energy that comes not only from your brain cells but from your entire body – can attract like vibrations. Wouldn't you prefer to draw the energy of happiness or optimism instead of suffering or desperation? Do you expect to see light at the end of the tunnel or continued darkness? Your light may be attracting the light outside.

● ● ●

My oldest brother loved food – everything about food. Eating it, smelling it, cooking it, he loved it all. He was very ill towards the end of his life, and it pained me to see him unable to eat as a result of complications from cancer. But he watched food shows on television with my mother in his final weeks. He said it helped him to imagine he could still taste the delicious food that was created on the shows. Although he knew he wasn't tasting the food, imagining that he was eating it was almost as good, and it made him happy. He chose to create happiness in his final days by thinking and imagining the things that made him smile.

I remember looking at my skeleton of a brother and saying to myself that if I could take on his cancer for him and alleviate his pain, I would, because I loved him so much. Was I asking for cancer? No, not in my mind. I was simply asking for relief for my brother.

Two years later, I was diagnosed with breast cancer. Did I wish it upon myself? Probably not. Would I have remained cancer-free had I not said that to myself when my brother was dying? I highly doubt it. The cancer was most likely a product of my environment, my genetics, stress, or other pre-determined experience I agreed upon before becoming alive.

But here's the thing. The "how" doesn't matter.

•   •   •

I could have second guessed my situation over and over again, but why? Now is what matters. At the moment I was diagnosed with cancer, I told the doctor that I was already healing. I was on my way to being cancer-free. I embraced my own body, knowing that the mass inside my breast was simply a ball of misguided cells, and if all my cells were created from energy, then couldn't I help realign the energy of my own body? He was skeptical and told me the odds of this type of cancer. My response was that the odds didn't matter – what mattered was how I perceived the event.

You will have things happen. This is why you are here in this lifetime, in your special, beautifully imperfect body. You are here to experience pain and love, and to taste, smell, hear, touch, and see your existence in form. To experience limits, such as time and space, matter and mind. Your focus is now – not to second guess or analyze how, why, or if you were dealt the cards you were dealt. By focusing on the now and making conscious choices through thought and action, you can create your future. You can play the game. You can buy as many red hotels as you want, and you can cross the finish line – backwards, in a neon green tutu, if you choose.

* * *

Instead of worrying, ask the question, "How can I make the most of my time here, right now, despite my circumstances? How do I want to feel now? Do I want to continue to worry and wring my hands over past choices, or shall I move forward with clear, loving choices?"

When you become ill, you might wonder if you created it. If you face difficult circumstances or find yourself in an unhealthy relationship, you might ask if it is your fault. Did you allow it? You probably won't know how your environment and your beliefs may have contributed to your health. But you have the power inside you to focus on healing.

Environmental stresses can knock the body out of balance. When a person hears a prognosis, he or she might begin immediately to believe it.

You may not be able to change the diagnosis, but you might be able to change the prognosis.

● ● ●

At the time of my diagnosis, I knew instinctively that I was in control of my prognosis. I knew I couldn't push the river. I could either float along with it and enjoy the view, navigate the rough water with free will and choice, or get out of the boat altogether and start swimming. Complaining wouldn't help.

Your thoughts, your beliefs, and your emotions can affect your healing. You have more power to heal yourself than you might ever believe is possible. Thinking, emotions, beliefs could cause biological or chemical reactions and changes in the body. Your beliefs can shift your biology, repair, and redirect.

Group thought can bring on healing, too. If one thought has infinite possibilities, then group focus on one outcome must add more power to the soup, don't you think? It is a transcendental force. This is what prayer is: a thought from one person or many, that creates a vibration of love to attract like vibrations and manifest an outcome. The idea of prayer, group meditation, or any cooperative thought process is beyond a singular religion and does not require religion or people of the same religion to manifest. Love is love is love.

●   ●   ●

And your results are your own. In *Gregg Braden – The Science of Miracles: The Quantum Language of Healing, Peace & Miracles*, Braden shares an experience in the early 1990s. He tells of a woman who had been diagnosed with a 3-inch cancerous tumor, and had been told it was inoperable. She decided to go to a medicine-free hospital in Beijing, where she learned about changes she could make in her life, and how to let go of the idea that she was ill, and instead look at her body as healing. Practitioners then used energy work in concert to help facilitate the healing of the tumor. A split screen ultrasound showed how the tumor responded to their chants, disappearing within three minutes. "Every organ has the ability to heal itself, given the right circumstances," explains Braden in the film *Heal*.

You may think such an event is impossible, that no group of people could ever get rid of a tumor by chanting words of affirmation. But you might be willing to join others in prayer to ask for healing of a loved one or hold a vigil to send "thoughts and prayers" to a missing person. Prayer is merely an avenue of thought, and traditional masses, gatherings, or prayer circles are powerful energetic rockets of thought.

●　●　●

Mastermind groups for businesses operate on the same principle. Many minds bring about great ideas when properly channeled. Even connecting with other minds through thought itself can bring about new ideas and processes.

I wanted to create a mastermind group of my own a few years ago, but I wanted a collective of great minds who had track records of achievement. After struggling to find people of like mind in my area, I decided to create an imagined mastermind group – one that existed only in my imagination and included people I had admired from afar. I made a list of people who showed skills or character traits I wanted to emulate. And the list was eclectic – Phyllis Diller, Warren Buffett, Bob Proctor, and Bob Newhart were part of my "pretend" mastermind group.

Some had already passed on, but I still included them in the list, with the belief that they were now an energetic part of The Knowing and had even more pull. I reached out to those who were still experiencing being alive, and connected with a few of them on internet sites. To the ones who accepted those invitations, I replied and told them about my imaginary group. It may have seemed a little "over the top" to them, as I never received an answer from any of them. But it didn't matter. I am now forever connected to them through my imaginary thought group, and I use their stories to create action steps of my own.

●　●　●

You might worry about so many things that you don't have control over – the weather, taxes, traffic. Those are all things that are either natural occurrences or have been created, managed, and controlled by others. But they become huge topics of conversation. At the same time you might avoid thinking about, and acting on, things you can control – your behavior, your procrastination, or your habits.

What things do you worry about but have no control over? How can you flip your thoughts to ways you could alleviate the worry? Use FEAR to guide you through. Could you take steps to lessen the worry in some way?

PRACTICE

Do you find yourself sad over the news or feeling a bit grumpy over a challenging day? Do you share all your aches and pains or whine about the latest news flash? You are not alone – we all do it from time to time. But instead of falling into the complain game, think about ways you can look at it in a different way. Having trouble? Sometimes it is easier to see the negativity of others, so use it to your advantage. When you hear someone complain, practice by coming up with ways that person could become more positive (I would suggest you do this privately – some beings are not ready to have others help, and they should be allowed to change on their own). Once you have mastered the technique by being an armchair quarterback, move on to your own statements of woe!

SUMMARY

- You are in complete control of your reaction to a trauma or event.
- We are here to experience all things including emotion, and to experience limits such as time and space, matter and mind.
- Groups offer greater, more powerful thoughts and create amazing results.
- Our thoughts, our beliefs, our emotions can affect our healing.

CHAPTER 7: THE ROLE OF EMOTION ON OUR THOUGHTS

You choose to experience emotions at the moment you step into that canoe of your own, at the very beginning of your journey into a linear existence. Does emotion guide your thoughts, or do thoughts navigate your emotions? Does thought always come from a consciousness outside yourself? Your emotions can help you create or destroy your surroundings, your relationships, and your health. Thought and emotion go hand in hand and are partners from the same energy that help you find purpose.

●　●　●

In his 2015 paper, *Heart-Brain Neurodynamics: The Making of Emotions*, Dr. Rollin McCraty, director of research for HeartMath Institute, states that there is a two-way communication between the emotional system and the cognitive system. But the number of neural connections going from the emotional processing areas is greater.

"This goes some way to explain the powerful

influence of emotions on thought processes. It also provides insight into how emotional experience, in contrast to thought alone, can often be a powerful motivator of future attitudes and behavior, influencing moment-to-moment actions as well as both short-term and long-term performance," Dr. McCraty writes. "While emotions can easily dispel non-emotional events from conscious awareness, non-emotional forms of mental activity, such as thoughts, do not so easily displace emotions from the mental landscape. Likewise, experience reminds us that the most pervasive thoughts, least easily dismissed, are typically those fueled by the greatest intensity of emotion."

So if you are practicing purposeful thinking, but your emotional state is still in turmoil, it might be more difficult or even impossible to shift your outlook to change your outcome. Your emotions can cause you to continue thinking about a problem or event. You might be sad about something and your thoughts continually turn back to the event. This creates a vibration of confusion, and The Knowing moves to match those vibrations. But creating a new event that makes you happy or exuberant could also serve to loop happy thoughts in your mind.

●   ●   ●

Does faking a desired emotion help? Dr. Mc-Craty suggests in his paper that there is a distinct connection between the mental and emotional systems, and if the two are not synchronized, they conflict with each other. "For example, people commonly tell themselves to 'think positive' about a challenging task, yet emotionally they may still dread doing it. When our emotions are not aligned with getting the task accomplished, we lack motivation and enthusiasm, which limits our access to creativity and insight, and thus impedes our overall performance."

If this is true, then it is important to understand the emotion as much as it is important to think and intend in a purposeful way.

If you are a human, then you have emotions – it is, in my opinion, a sense that allows you to experience the other prominent five senses on a different level. And even the emotions that you perceive as bad ones are not really bad at all. You will feel so-called "negative" emotions such as anger or sadness, no matter how settled you are in your happiness canoe.

The key is to understand and accept them, discover what the emotions are truly about, and learn how to move through them with positive intention.

• • •

Sometimes you might have an emotional reaction to an event or to a deep-seated trigger from your past. This might be a natural response to a death or loss of some kind, a trauma, or the actions of another person. Then you have a second emotional response - one that is a reaction to that first emotion. You might start to feel guilty over not communicating with a now-deceased loved one, or remorse over a mistake you once made. Perhaps you judge yourself after a person has been angry towards you. The first emotional reaction is often short-lived and easy to maneuver. But the second one might hang on for a while, causing you to replay an episode in your mind, or play the "what if" game with yourself. You get stuck in the emotional hamster wheel. You keep expending energy to get nowhere, and you obsess over every detail of an event or interaction. The good thing is, the second one is within your power to control – you can choose how to manage it.

●   ●   ●

In the article, "Modulation of DNA Conformation by Heart-Focused Intention" (McCraty, Atkinson,Tomasino, 2003), researchers describe experiments that show that our DNA can be influenced by human intention.

In one experiment, an individual holding three DNA samples was directed to create a state of mental, emotional, and physical harmony using a HeartMath technique that includes intentional positive emotions. That individual managed to unwind two of the three DNA samples and leave the third sample unchanged, which was the intention. The article states that "...when individuals are in a heart-focused, loving state and in a more coherent mode of physiological functioning, they have a greater ability to alter the conformation of DNA."

DNA can be altered? Yes.

Your emotions and thoughts can change the physical conformation of DNA.

Remember the studies involving the effect of

positive and negative speech on plants? It is true that your energy, your emotional state, is a powerful tool to heal, to grow, and to access infinite possibility.

● ● ●

The first step is to acknowledge the emotion. Turning to FEAR (Face Every Anxious Reflex) instead of turning away to run from fear, you can see that the emotion isn't really that big a deal. It's like the little puffer fish that fills himself up with air to look more intimidating – but really, it's just a lot of air.

Where does this emotion come from? What is this feeling really about? Is it truly a reaction to the event you just experienced, or is it a reminder of something that happened long ago?

Acknowledge the emotions you are feeling, but don't hang on to them. Don't rehearse the bad stuff like you are practicing for a stage play. Know that it is energy, just like everything else, and it can be changed into a form that is more useful. That doesn't mean you have to act on the emotion – simply sit with it for a time and understand that the reaction is not you. You have more to do than to stay on the hamster wheel, and when you are ready, all you have to do is stop running, and jump off.

•   •   •

Your heart plays a part not only in your ability to stay alive; it is an integral piece of the puzzle of your purpose. To allow thought to manifest in a productive and loving way, it must align with the heart to access The Knowing.

"Some people consider thought as equivalent with consciousness, which I don't," Dr. McCraty says. "...what I'm suggesting is that there is another dimension of our wholeness that exists in another level of density, another dimension - what people call their higher self or their larger self, spirit or soul, depending on their culture or belief system - suggesting that it has real structure."

Dr. McCraty continues, "That flow of information from that level of our beingness, of our undivided wholeness, is accessed through the energetic heart, which can be thought of as a main computer that transforms the information from the higher dimensional self down into the DNA and mind/brain systems of the human body. And as we access more to that aspect of our deep self, it elevates or lifts our consciousness or awareness, which upgrades our emotions, thoughts, and behaviors. That's what the shift that people are talking about is all about."

PRACTICE

If you find yourself feeling aggravated or even angry while driving, practice the SODA method:

Stop – Stop what you are doing for a moment, and take in some deep breaths. Bring yourself back to the present by breathing deep into your chest, focusing on the rise and fall of your chest.

Observe – What are you thinking of or focusing on? Where did these feelings come from – the current problem or one that is in the past? How is your body handling this emotion?

Decide – Decide how you would like to feel. What is the end result you would like to experience? Determine a more suitable way of moving forward.

Act – Take action. Taking even the smallest of steps will help you break through that reflex. What

can you do that better matches your desired outcome and fits your ethics and values? What can you
do to climb back into the happiness canoe?

SUMMARY

- Information from our being is accessed through the
  energetic heart and transfers down into the mind/brain/
  human body.
- As we elevate our awareness, our thoughts, behavior,
  and emotions change as well.
- So if you are practicing purposeful thinking, but your
  emotional state is still in turmoil, it might be more
  difficult or even impossible to shift your outlook to
  change your outcome.
- You should acknowledge and understand the emotion
  in order to think and intend in a purposeful way.
- Using the SODA method can help you align your
  emotions with your thoughts.

CHAPTER 8: IMAGINING AND THE BRAIN

Knowing how your goal will manifest is not important. In fact, it could slow the process. Your result is a feeling – happiness, contentment, achievement, joy, bliss. It can manifest in many different ways, not just in the achievement of a specific goal. Intending a broader outcome on an emotional level will allow more opportunities to present themselves to you. So if your wish is for happiness, create the feeling of happiness in your brain.

Imagining can also be a powerful tool to strengthen the mind/body connection. And, as you learned in the last chapter, a connection with the heart, the brain, and the outside sources of energy is important in purposeful thought.

● ● ●

Renowned soprano Renee Fleming, a 2013 National Medal of Arts winner and artistic advisor to the Kennedy Center, recently participated in a brain experiment. The opera star had partnered with NIH Director, geneticist and musician Dr. Francis Collins to start the Sound Health initiative. Called *Sound Health: Music and the Mind*, the initiative is a partnership between the NIH and the John F. Kennedy Center for the Performing Arts in Washington D.C. The initiative takes a look at how listening to, performing, or creating music involves the brain, in the hopes that the brain can be managed to improve mental and physical health.

Fleming was scanned inside an MRI machine at the National Institute of Health (NIH) campus. In the study, she was given three different instructions for her time in the MRI machine: to sing, to imagine singing, and to listen to music.

In Fleming's case, several brain regions were found to be more active when she imagined singing than when she actually sang aloud. Her amygdala, occipital cortex, frontal cortex, motor cortex and other parts of the brain fired up while she imagined singing. The amygdala plays a role in processing emotion – Fleming sang a song that evoked emotion, and the act of imagining singing may have made the amygdala work harder to maintain the emotion. Not only did she ignite the parts of the brain that control timing, complicated thinking and keeping track of tasks and schedules, but she also signaled the emotion center and areas involved with motion and vision.

Scientists believed that it took more effort to imagine herself on stage, singing, than it did to actually physically perform.

So it seems that imagination can actually help some parts of the brain fire and communicate with other parts of the brain. This could in turn strengthen the mind/body connection and allow healing to occur.

In Fleming's case, imagining the act of singing on stage activated the brain in a way that listening to song or physically singing could not do. Thought powers the mind.

•   •   •

Thought also powers more than your physical body. Going back to the idea that thought lies within and beyond the confines of the box of logic and physical reality, then it would be fair to say that thought includes other boxes as well. It is a system of communication between all the boxes and all the spaces in between.

If you try to mold it into your most acceptable way of thinking, it doesn't fit. It fills the box and everything around it. And it becomes the box itself. The energy of thought constantly moves and shifts.

"In a Universe whose basic nature is Holistic and Holographic, that is, comprised of whole systems interconnected and interrelated, a nonlocal mind makes logical sense," Dianne Collins writes in her book, *Do You QuantumThink?: New Thinking That Will Rock Your World.* "If everything is connected as one whole, then in a very real way, even beyond the Internet, our minds are also interconnected – not just with one another, but with the whole of life."

With the whole of life! Is your mind blown yet? If you understand that your thoughts are connected with the whole of life, then you can also understand the thought of you, and how you can create a better life through purposeful thought.

* * *

If a person who imagines playing music can ignite fires in the brain that are more powerful than actually playing music, then what does this tell you? Thought is at the core of all creation and manifestation – that your thoughts can not only make an image in your mind, like the pink butterfly, but it can also change the very makeup of your brain and body and put you on a different path of wellness. It can manifest a different reality.

I shared the story of my brother, who imagined food and eating food by watching television programs. He was manifesting an emotion that helped him feel more comfortable. Instead of focusing on the fact that he could not eat, he decided to focus on how he could create the same comfort and feeling he got when he did eat. Instead of lack, he focused on satiety.

You can create an emotion of abundance that can change your outlook on your world, despite your circumstances.

No matter what your surroundings are, you can create and manifest a world of emotion. This is evident in many poverty stricken countries. People who have little to no resources still create happy homes and offer solace and shelter to others. They hold themselves in that happiness canoe, choosing to navigate their journey with confidence in their power.

* * *

Others choose to see lack despite their fortune. A wealthy CEO with a solid portfolio and a loving family might complain about all the taxes he must pay or the commute he has every morning. He insists that he is never given a break, that everyone is out to get him or take his money. He is jealous of his wife, and only sees his children as obstacles that keep him from doing what he says is most important to him.

Perhaps that businessman learned how to do this by watching his father. His father was a hard-working man who rarely said anything while they ate at the dinner table. He allowed his wife to handle everyday problems, and all the physical and emotional needs of the children were the responsibility of the mother. The father's job was to put food on the table, to bring in money, to make everyone live comfortably on a material plane. His drive to succeed did not include happiness – it was about sustenance, responsibility, stigma, stature, and respect.

Or, the wealthy businessman had a different type of father and chose to go down the opposite path. Perhaps his father was a playful type, who favored time with his loved ones or the freedom to choose over a solid, reliable career. The father's wife may have nagged the father to do more to succeed, while complaining about the lack of money, the lack of material items, and the inability to keep up with the Joneses.

The wealthy businessman in fact saw his father as someone who disappointed his family. So he vowed to do more than his father. He decided to make as much money as possible, so his own family would never do without. He never wanted them to worry about hot water or food on the table. He succeeded in those things. But his belief over lack made him find ways to shield himself from thieves. He avoided letting go of money, loving too much, or playing too hard.

Those beliefs that you take on as a child by watching those around you play a part in how you act as an adult. It sometimes takes more than one try to understand why you do certain things.

• • •

A recent study examined how emotions and facial expressions influence athletes. Researchers from the University of Haifa and University of Amsterdam took a look at how a coach's expressions of anger or happiness influence the team's performance during a game.

They conducted two sub-studies among 30 baseball and softball teams, and 30 soccer teams. They found that expressions of happiness directed toward teams by their coaches – before the game began – increased the chances of leading the game by half-time. And the players' emotions mirrored the expressions of emotion – both anger and happiness – from the coach, regardless of the outcome of the game.

For years, coaches have used visualization techniques to help their teams succeed in games. Golfer Tiger Woods has used visualization techniques since he was a child. Heavyweight champion Muhammad Ali imagined himself "the greatest" boxer of all time and imagined his performance in the ring before every match.

● ● ●

I am still learning every day. I recently closed a blog that focused on debt reduction and saving money – something I learned from my own parents. They grew up in the Depression and learned how to live sparely – to use it up, wear it out, make it do, or do without. They scrimped and saved to make sure we all were fed. We were ensured of our needs being met, but not necessarily our wants. We learned how to handle circumstances – a good trait, for sure. But along the way, I took on this belief that I should live in lack – to have only the money that I need, but no more. That's what adults did, right? They used things up, wore things out, made things do, and did without.

I still believe that we should use things up and not waste. Wear things out before replacing them. Make it do in uncertain times. But that last one – do without. Who says we have to do without? Who says that because we are adults, we should resign ourselves to hardship? I wanted more from this time being alive. I wanted to experience as much as possible. I discontinued the blog with the intention that my focus would be on abundance instead of lack.

My new intention was on joyful days filled with rich experiences and opportunities. I manage my income in the best way possible, take care of my things so they will last as long as possible, and waste little so the planet can go on being the beautiful amazing sphere that I love so much. In fact, those first three phrases – use it up, wear it out, and make it do – are ways to show gratitude. And gratitude is a very important tool on this journey. We'll talk more about gratitude later.

● ● ●

Advertisements and commercials are constantly attacking your brain, telling you that you should be unsatisfied with your present situation. The peanut sellers want you to buy more peanuts, organizations want to give you tips on buying the perfect mattress that happens to be on sale this week, and companies tell you (in so many words) that you are a loser if you don't wear their clothing line or drink their special water.

The thoughts and beliefs of others can sway you and make you think that having these things will give you the elusive happiness – until they want to sell you the next thing.

Tickle Me Elmo, Cabbage Patch Dolls and Bean-ie Babies all caused chaos, sending parents to stand in long lines and take out money from their savings to buy them. The companies all used this tactic to make children and parents believe that if they didn't have that hot new toy, they were nothing on the playground. And if they did have the new toy, they were the envy of the third grade. But eventually, that giggling Elmo was a goner, and it was on to newer, better, faster.

But if you are refusing to follow the crowd, buy the best and newest, or choosing to use it up, wear it out, make it do because you think you can't afford to have any more than that, or if you think you are worth no more than what is right there in front of you – stop that thought right now. The last one – do without – is a dealbreaker. There is enough.

There is abundance just waiting for you to imagine and ask. There is as much as you can think there is.

• • •

The key is to re-imagine your circumstances. Think about everything you have access to as a wildly exciting treasure. Start to look at those simple, frugal meals as fantastic gourmet delights. I remember cooking bologna "daisies" for my sons during especially hard times. I imagined them to be fancy food items that could only be served on special occasions – and the boys went along with it. We celebrated the daisies. One of my sons still makes these low-cost food flowers every now and then, just to remind himself to be grateful for his past experiences and for his current one.

When you begin to practice the power of intentional thought, you will start influencing yourself instead of saving that job for others. You will have more trust in yourself. You will start to see the opportunities and potential and focus on the things you hold as valuable.

● ● ●

You must remember, in your quest to understand the power of thought, that you should not beg for something when you are intending or act as if getting it is beyond the scope of your thought. The earth-plane requests fall by the wayside pretty quickly when something bigger needs our attention. Keep your focus on what is most important. Stop questioning the level of your power.

In the imagining brain, you can become whatever you want – and The Knowing takes that as a go-ahead to start matching that vision. If you believe you are destined to experience lack, you will experience lack.

Sometimes the belief that you have is shrouded in a cloak of tradition or culture or social structure. Who do you think you are? That is a question you may have heard when you decided to push the envelope. "That just isn't done," they say. But why not? Give me a reason why you can't have more – will you will be causing harm by having a happy life?

I am certainly not saying you should harm anyone in the attainment of whatever you are imagining. The Knowing offers a nonjudgmental support system, but at the core of it is love. If your intention is not based on love, then it is based on lack. So ask yourself why you would offer lack of any form if you want to attain abundance.

Taking from others or causing harm to others is creating lack – and counterproductive to your intention. Think of loving experiences and non-exclusive situations that create a ripple-out effect of abundance. By giving, you receive. By taking in any way other than love, you experience loss. Your thoughts become matter – and they matter.

PRACTICE

Take a few moments before working out, running, or beginning a task. Imagine yourself performing this task with ease, and with a positive outcome. For instance, if you are running, imagine that you will run a half-mile farther than your most difficult distance, and you will run with ease and at a somewhat faster pace. Imagine the natural high, the emotion that comes with a successful run. In your mind, pump the air and dance a bit after your imagined run.

Then notice how it affects your actual performance.

SUMMARY

- If your wish is for happiness, create the feeling of happiness in your brain.
- Imagination can actually help some parts of the brain fire and communicate with other parts of the brain.
- Imagining a process and outcome could strengthen the mind/body connection and allow healing to occur.
- If you understand that your thoughts are connected with the whole of life, then you can also understand how you can create your life through thought.
- When you begin to practice the power of intentional thought, you will start influencing yourself instead of saving that job for others. You will have more trust in yourself. You will start to see the opportunities and potential and focus on the things you hold as valuable.
- If your intention is not based on love, then it is based on lack.

CHAPTER 9: ALIGNING YOUR THOUGHTS TO MATCH YOUR INTENT

How can you align your thoughts to create a better future?

Your physical body is loaded with thought, and your heart, head, mind, arms, and legs are all tuned in to it. You are also connected to thought outside your body from The Knowing and from other energetic beings who are alive, and you are already tapped into it. You have free will to use and manipulate thought in whatever way you choose.

Evidence is sometimes not attached to belief. Skeptics ask, where is the evidence? Scientists can theorize about many things, but can't prove them yet – in the past, they couldn't prove that the world was round. Scientists are quickly learning that as soon as they learn one thing, more things pop up to be discovered. As their knowledge expands, so does their world.

As we know, we grow.

•   •   •

If you find reasons to discount what I am saying anywhere in this book, I'm okay with that. Go ahead. I'm not here to twist your arm or force you to believe anything.

And the cool thing is you don't have to believe it for it to work.

You can say air isn't real or the internet isn't real or space isn't real. Because it all keeps working whether you believe in it or not. This idea can be applied to you and your physical being, complete with mind and heart. If someone finds a reason to discount your goals, understand that you have the power to go ahead, whether they believe you or not. You are a force.

Thought cannot be measured or bagged – but you know that you think. You can't hold it, or see it before it takes form in your mind, you can't put a ring on it. It is limitless. And if belief is exclusionary, it may not be truth. Universal laws such as gravity and the law of attraction are relevant to everyone. You are not stuck to the earth through gravity because you are of a certain faith, or live in a certain community, or wear a certain shoe size. And you are not excluded from this power of thought – *you are thought*. The energy that is you is part of the The Knowing, and it is up to you how it all plays out.

● ● ●

Take a moment to consider this – if indeed you believed that thought is a grand energetic force inside you and outside you, and you wanted to rec-reate your goals, how would you do it? If you want to blow out a candle, what do you do? If you want to swim to an island in the middle of the lake, what do you do? If you want to make a cake, what do you do?

You think about it first. You imagine the result – the extinguished candle, sitting on that island in the middle of the lake, or the just-baked chocolat-ey goodness of a two-layer cake. You see the end result in your mind.

Then thought continues and tells your brain to take action. You draw in a breath to blow out the candle, you step into the water of the lake, or you start to gather the cake ingredients.

The actions allow you to propel forward to the goal.

But now, I ask you this: If you want happiness, what do you do?

●   ●   ●

You do exactly the same thing.

But, you say, how can I envision happiness? What does it look like?

It looks like cake and islands and candles. It looks like romance and success and wealth. It looks like whatever you want. But to keep on manifesting the stuff of your dreams, you must allow it to take on a bigger form than material things. If you don't, you are simply jumping from one small thing to another, never completely satisfied, and always searching for another cake or island or candle. The bigger form it must take is a feeling. It is the thing that fills your heart, the canoe, the wave of emotion that takes over your body and your eyes and your throat, and makes you weep with joy or grief. It is the sense that no one has added to the fabulous five – taste, touch, smell, sound, sight – because it is bigger and smarter and more transcendent than all of them. It is directly connected to The Knowing.

I would like you to think about the emotions you would feel when you accomplish that goal.

How does happiness feel?

When you think about the feeling, you might immediately get a rush of energy – perhaps you see yourself smiling, and you begin to smile. Maybe you think about jumping in the air, spinning around in circles, or grabbing a loved one and hugging him tightly. If you see a past event, focus on the feeling you had then, not on the event itself.

●   ●   ●

Maybe happiness for you takes a form of serenity or quiet. Zen Master and spiritual leader Thich Nhat Hanh says this:

"Many people think excitement is happiness.... But when you are excited you are not peaceful. True happiness is based on peace."

Whatever form it takes, allow the thought of happiness and the visions it creates in your mind to fill your entire body, to experience the "music" of happiness just as Renee Fleming experienced a surge of energy in her brain when she simply thought about music. Did you find yourself smiling? Did you feel your body relax a bit, or did you feel a tingling in your limbs?

The true goal is in the canoe. To experience the canoe, you must get in it first. And then paddle.

●   ●   ●

You have control over your thoughts, but you also learn to allow and trust the outside forces.

You can hold on and let go at the same time.

Once you have determined your goal – your desired emotion – and you have created the thought – the intention – and taken action steps to attain it (smiling, feeling the feeling, taking action steps), The Knowing takes hold of that thought and vibrates to match it, creating opportunity and circumstance that matches your thought and intention.

●   ●   ●

If you try to micromanage the larger picture, the focus becomes narrower, harder to complete.

Energy can bottleneck, and by perceiving a specific outcome, the natural flow is slowed. But if you offer a thought of emotion, then release it to The Knowing, you allow synchronicity, you allow flow, you allow situations that you would never have dreamed of to surface. Your outcome may not look anything like your narrow picture, but it is perfect.

Let's imagine that your big picture intent is happiness. You make your intention, feel the emotion, and then send it off to The Knowing to be processed and returned. But...you decide that the *only* way you will be happy is if you have a career as a CEO of a large Fortune 500 company. You then insist that The Knowing find exactly that situation for you. Immediately, the wheels begin to turn, and The Knowing sets situations in motion that will give you opportunities to become a CEO in a Fortune 500 company. It is a much slower process, because the intent is streamlined and must align with the predetermined realities of others.

But years later, it happens.

There! You made it! Happiness!

You begin to realize that this job isn't what you thought it was. It has not only taken up a lot of your time, but you also have no time to enjoy your family. You drop out of your bowling league because you have to stay late at work. You no longer jump out of bed in the morning to get to your shiny corner office.

You are no longer happy.

You wonder, why didn't The Knowing offer happiness?

Because you didn't really ask for happiness. You asked for a certain role in a company.

The big picture disappeared in the minute details you placed. You jumped out of the happiness canoe and into the water to grasp at a piece of driftwood that floated by.

That job was not your happiness. Your happiness is your purpose. And your happiness looks completely different from mine or anyone else's.

"Most people ask, 'What's my purpose?' And

once they see it, it just makes it more matter-of-fact," says Dianne Collins. "Then because purpose evolves and keeps expanding, you keep looking. You keep seeing it and distinguishing it in ever-new ways, and that's the fun of the game of life, right? You could come into this incarnation with a certain talent, and then never develop it or use it. However, when you see your special gifts, you know they are yours to express and give to the world. That is so satisfying. It's actually exhilarating!"

You are probably thinking that this is becoming very complex. After all, you *are* thought. So it should be much easier, right? You are tired already, and you haven't even finished the book.

The truth is, it is ridiculously easy.

•   •   •

You might wake up one morning and feel "off" and say to yourself, I must be coming down with something. I don't feel right. The rest of the day, you offer that excuse – you say to your boss that you are just not feeling well, that you must be coming down with a cold or the flu.

You're not on your game. You increase the vibration that matches the belief that you are ill. In fact, you are right – you come down with the flu or a cold. You don't feel well.

Let's say you got up and felt that little twinge of unwellness, but instead said to yourself, "I am already healing," "I am feeling better with this extra vitamin C," or "I am healthy and happy." What if you continued stating the optimistic point of view for the rest of the day, instead of the doomsday view? Would it change things? Only you can find that out. At the very least, you will raise the vibration of your mood to a happier place, as well as affect the others around you in a different way.

You are aligning your thoughts every moment, and every moment brings a vibration that could manifest into form. The more you practice keeping your thoughts on a consistent level, the more you will see the results. Your energy draws like energy, so be ready to flip the record to the optimistic side.

●　●　●

Please don't start thinking that you are not allowed or able to manifest small, earth-based things –

because you are. You can manifest a clean toothpick or a forest of hardwoods. The forest might take more or less time than the toothpick. By all means, work on the little things every day, because not only do they make you smile, but they also serve as exercises for your thoughts.

Several years ago, I remember driving with a friend down a Washington highway, that was packed with cars. We were crawling along, and my friend said something like, "We'll never get there on time!" and she pointed out the window at the cars in front of us. I remember saying "We are on our way! The traffic is moving along, and it is parting the way for us!" I gave a dramatic wave, like Moses parting the Red Sea. Instantly, the cars ahead of us moved to other lanes, and the flow of traffic sped up. We had a clear lane ahead of us, and quickly made the speed limit again. My friend laughed about the manifestation – but we both knew that it wasn't coincidence.

● ● ●

The more you purposely manifest things, the more you believe you can. Your beliefs are what fuel the intentions – and sometimes subconsciously you believe one thing and ask to manifest another.

How many times have you thought about how nice it would be to win the lottery? But then you think, who are you kidding? You can't win the lottery – the odds are ridiculously high, and it never happens to people who would know how to put that money to its best and more purposeful use. It always goes to someone who will fritter it away until they are worse off than before they won the lottery.

Let's talk about those people first – the ones who win and then lose all the money. They are living out their own limited belief – that money never comes easy. That money is evil. That rich people are evil. If they are rich, they might be evil, so quick! Somebody take this money before I am corrupted by it!

Okay, let's go back to you. You say you can't even win the lottery, let alone get a chance to spend it. Money doesn't just fly in the window like that, at least for you. You never get opportunities like that. So because you have just told yourself off over the idea of winning the lottery, you don't even bother to buy a ticket. Sealing your fate that indeed, you will never win the lottery.

Or you might take the step to buy a ticket. You then worry over the numbers, in order to match the winning numbers that will be pulled. But if you truly believe you can win the lottery, why would you agonize over the choice of numbers? Wouldn't you just buy a ticket and allow The Knowing to align the lottery draw to match the numbers on your ticket?

I can hear you – she hasn't won any lotteries herself, now, has she? And you would be right. I'm a work in progress. I can work up the belief and then second guess the possibility. The Knowing chases after the thought, sniffs it, and then goes after the juicier, thicker, more experienced thought that I'm incapable of winning a six-figure prize. But I have manifested some pretty awesome things in my life – enough to know that it works, whether we are aware of the desire or not.

●   ●   ●

The law of attraction works whether you know about it or not. It is a truth – and if you think you have to join some fanatical new world order, wear a special uniform, or stop eating beef for it to work properly, you would be wrong. You didn't even have to buy this book. But you did – which, by the way, means my own intentions are working.

To tap into the power of thought, you have to start here. State your purpose and focus on it. Then take some action steps.

Are you in a stagnant job and want more out of your career? Create the image of your wish, and ask for it to manifest. Make your decisions based on that dream. Bring it into the present, which means you start acting as if you already are in the perfect job. Think about how wonderful your job is and how happy you are. Pretend that you are already in that perfect job and bring that act to your current work. Come in every day with a smile on your face, tell yourself that every task you have at work is something you are not only brilliant at, but you really have fun doing it. Bring on the happy.

●　●　●

You might feel a little vulnerable or even silly by creating this success in your mind. Your co-workers might check the top drawer of your desk to see if you've been taking a nip every now and then. You might even begin to feel as if you are doing something wrong by secretly intending a better job. How dare you think so big? Who are you to think you can do better? You might imagine coworkers saying, "He thinks he is too good for us. What is he hiding? Why is he so happy?"

Those statements have nothing to do with you. The people who make those statements are speaking from fear. Change, any change, is scary and maybe intimidating to them. How can you be so happy working in a thankless, miserable job? If you succeed, then why aren't they able to do the same thing? How can they discover the secret sauce and move forward without leaving every excuse or belief behind?

They can, just like you are doing right now. Fear can become FEAR. The key is to shoot for the emotion – and then you are where you want to be. And just like that, the world is at your feet.

● ● ●

Have fun manifesting small things and finding great parking spots. But use them as practice sessions. Don't stay in that batter's box forever, hitting balls against the wall. The goal is to step out on the field and knock that bat against the plate, raise your elbows, and hit it out of the park.

This moment, this now, is the most important time of your life. The tenth-century poet Omar Khayyam said, "Be happy for this moment. This moment is your life."

The "things" are great. But remember that canoe analogy. If you fill your canoe with driftwood that serves only to cramp your navigating style, your journey becomes a chore. Hiding out in the canoe filled with weighted junk is a way to keep from journeying at all. Don't get caught up in the fear of success. You are successful now, manifesting whatever you are focusing on. So why not have more fun with it? Start intending good things. Every thought you have has a vibrational match, and it will form in some way. The more you practice streamlining the intention, the more visible the manifestation.

PRACTICE

State and create your larger intentions. Imagine them as if they are already happening. But practice on a day-to-day basis by intending smaller accomplishments. Intend quicker elevators, open parking spots, a sale on that blouse you've been admiring. It's okay to desire material things, as long as they are not your primary goal. Hone your skills in purposeful thought while you are working on larger opportunities.

SUMMARY

- We can't hold thought in our hands or see it before it takes form in our minds. It is limitless.
- Universal laws such as gravity and the law of attraction are relevant to everyone.
- You are not stuck to the earth through gravity because you are of a certain faith or heritage.
- And you are not excluded from this power of thought – you *are* thought.
- You can control your thoughts and beliefs by consciously changing them
- You are aligning your thoughts every moment, and every moment brings a vibration that could manifest into form.

CHAPTER 10: VISUALIZATION AND EMOTI-BOARDS

Now that you are more familiar with the idea of thought, imagining, and the heart/mind connection, you can create a visual representation of your purpose.

You've probably heard of vision boards. You cut out and paste a picture of a sandy beach, a loving couple, and a pile of cash onto the vision board, thinking that your life would be changed if you receive these things. But you might still doubt the possibility that they will appear. You use the vision board workshops as a way to mingle with other dreamers, to drink wine and lament over your lives, bemoaning that you are broke, single, sad, or stuck in a rut.

The idea of visualization is great, and vision boards can definitely help you. As you learned in the previous chapters, imagining and creating visions of our intended goals is an important part of manifesting a more fulfilling life. But you also learned that the emotion must be there – the feeling of accomplishing that goal, purchasing that perfect house, or finding that great relationship.

I suggest that you create a similar board, but one that will go deeper than the shallow representations of desires often expressed with vision boards.

These boards are what I call Emoti-Boards.

* * *

Emoti-Boards represent what you really desire – not the cars, houses, piles of money, or even the long lazy days on the beach. The Emoti-Board represents the emotion you think those things will bring to you.

You want to feel the emotion first, then think of the objects or opportunities that emotion might bring to you.

You want a new car because you will feel successful. You want to be successful because you want more money. You want money so you can make your lives and the lives of your loved ones more comfortable. You want to be more comfortable so you can experience more things, and enjoy yourself.

You want those things so you can be happy.

But now you know that happiness is not the end result and shouldn't be considered the light at the end of the tunnel. The "things" won't bring happiness.

Instead, happiness brings the "things."

You are the light at the end of the tunnel. You hold happiness inside you, right now. What you are searching for is already inside you.

Once you pull that happiness light out of your pocket, The Knowing starts lining up opportunities to keep you at that happiness vibration. It is the law of attraction, the pull that is as strong and true as gravity itself. If you vibrate happiness, you attract happiness in its many forms.

Let's go back for a moment, to that long river of life that was described in an earlier chapter. That river is long and winding or short and straight. It might have twists and turns, quiet pools and raging rapids. You want to travel that river of life because you created most of it before you became alive.

You decided your purpose and how you would experience it, how much of The Knowing you would forget so you could play with everything that was offered. Do you jump in and swim your way through, sometimes just struggling to keep your head above water? Or do you choose a canoe at the beginning – one that will allow you to stay secure and dry and able to navigate the waters using the paddles of free will and choice?

Your canoe is right there, waiting for you – beautiful, life-worthy, and shining with stardust.

You can now get in your canoe and push off into the river. No matter how crazy that river of life gets, you can stay in that vessel. Lucky you! You paddle and navigate the river with your free will and choice, and you choose to stop along the way and have adventures and encounters. The river is loaded with opportunity that floats along like driftwood, swims like animals or fish, or hangs over your head like the branches of a willow tree. You get to pick what you want to carry along with you.

Your Emoti-Board will illustrate your journey by beginning with the canoe – the emotion – you want to ride in while you navigate the river of life.

● ● ●

Before you get on to the business of creating an Emoti-Board, let's take a look at how the board can help you manifest your desires.

Perhaps you would like to be rich. But you look at a person who is already wealthy, and you begin to judge him (or her). You think to yourself, it's easy for him to do these things – he is rich. He should share more of his money. Boy, he is greedy. He has let all that money go to his head.

Underneath those thoughts is the belief that money has caused this person to become greedy, thoughtless, selfish, and shallow. Money is therefore an evil entity. Your subconscious says, I can't have money, or I will become greedy or selfish. I will be judged by people just as I am judging the wealthy. I don't want that. I don't want money.

In order to propel your wish to be rich, you must embrace the idea that money is good.

Remember, money is simply an exchange of

energy – and it is the *intent* behind the exchange
of money that matters, as is the character of the
human being. Money only serves as a tool to create
personal worlds and enhances the character of the
person who uses it. Those worlds deserve no judg-
ment and are solely the concern of the people who
create them.

When you begin the process of creating an
Emoti-Board, pay attention to your thoughts about
money, relationships, health, careers, etc. If you find
you are limiting your ability to create in one or more
areas, change your thoughts to a more positive
statement.

For instance, you may say to yourself, "I don't
know why I am asking for a great career. I can only
go so far in this business." Reframe that statement
into a more positive, open-ended request, such as, "I
am open to receiving opportunities to improve and
break through career ceilings."

You may hope to find a romantic partner, but
you hear yourself say, "I don't want any more losers."
Well, that's no way to find a great partner! Flip that
record to the other side. Say something like, "I am

ready to accept a kind and loving partner into my world." You get the picture – turn negatives into positives, and repeat those new thoughts until they are habits.

Emoti-Boards (and vision boards) are extensions and forms of thought. You think about what you desire and expand on that thought by making statements, searching for appropriate pictures to illustrate the thought, and focusing on the creation of the board itself.

James A. Ray, author of *The Science of Success: How to Attract Prosperity and Create Life Balance*, calls his vision boards "dream boards." He states that his dream board is filled with images of places he'd like to go and things he would like to accomplish – and his dream board included a representation of the book he eventually wrote. He suggests making your own personal dream board full of vivid imagery and color – and to make the representations thoughtful and emotional.

The emotion holds hands with thought and imagination to begin a vibration that The Knowing will expand on and accessorize.

* * *

So let's begin:

Decide on a type of board that will be the base of your Emoti-Board. It might be poster board, or foam core. A cork board will allow you to pin images and phrases, move and remove them at will. A felt board on a wall might work in a meditation room, or you could draw as well tape your cut-out designs onto a chalkboard. A magnetized erasable board would give you some room for change. It's up to you.

Here is a list of other possible supplies, depending on your choice of board:

Tape
Glue
Scissors
Pushpins
Magnets
Sharpies
Erasable markers
Pencils and pens of different colors
Old magazines
Travel brochures

Family photos
Cards or invitations
Sentimental objects
Printed words and phrases
Stickers

Now before you start to cut out pictures of palm trees and pineapples, cars and companions, take a moment to close your eyes and imagine yourself in the world you plan to create. Think about the feeling you will have when you have successfully manifested your dreams. Are you feeling happiness, joy, or bliss? Contentment or security? Imagine a setting where you are engulfed in that feeling. You might be listening to the applause of a large audience or feeling the salty air of the ocean as you stand on a quiet beach. You might be surrounded by friends and family over a homemade feast. You decide.

Are you smiling? If not, make it happen. The act of smiling enhances the emotion.

● ● ●

Now, think of a word that describes that feeling.

That is your Emoti-Board canoe. This is where

you start to create your Emoti-Board.

Now search for ways to illustrate that feeling, and attach them to your board with the printed word.

If happiness is a walk on the beach, find an appropriate picture, and overlay it with the word "Happiness." Joy might come in the form of children playing together or dolphins jumping and diving into an open sea. The illustration is merely a meta-phor for the feeling you have captured. The picture is the music that accompanies a movie scene.

The simple act of experiencing that emotion, finding a picture and phrase to illustrate the emo-tion, and purposefully attaching it to the board, cre-ates a vibration that is sent out to The Knowing, to the larger version of you – the part of you that exists beyond the body and mind in which you currently reside. Every vibration you create through thought attracts like vibrations in the form of opportunities, people, items, and events.

You could stop right there, and you would see results from your board. But you want to enhance the vibration with other representations of happiness. Consider the position of your emotional phrase as the center of your board, with everything radiating from that center. That emotion is the beginning of your journey, as well as the end result. You create your vision board around the emotion you choose.

We will use Happiness as our central emotion for the purposes of this book, but please use whatever emotional phrase that works best for you.

●   ●   ●

Now, let's look at the subcategories of that emotion. We can divide them into five primary groups: health, abundance, career or livelihood, relationships, and appearances.

Divide the rest of your board into 5 sections, each representing one of the groups listed above. You could draw lines that radiate from the central emotion, spiral the groups out from the center, or create a design of your own. It should matter only to you. There is no right or wrong design.

After designating a group to each section, think

about things that you would like to manifest in each one. Let's take a look at health, for instance. You might want to include illustrations of fitness, healthy food, ideal weight, glowing skin, or something that will serve as a positive clue to some health issue you are working to correct. For instance, perhaps you are facing a cataract surgery – a picture of a clear and healthy eye would be a great choice.

Do you want to manifest a more lucrative career? Perhaps a photo of a corner office or even a person working on a laptop while lounging on a beach would do? Your career goals may involve travel, speaking, or writing in a secluded studio.

Take some time to think about what you really desire in each category, and look for ways to illustrate that scene without defining the actual job, automobile, or person you might currently have in mind. If you put your desires into a box, and forbid yourself to consider unknown options, you may overlook opportunities that do not "look" like what you expect. In fact, by allowing yourself to dream bigger, you learn to jump higher.

●　●　●

My son discovered this: After being fired from his "dream job," he let go of his own limiting beliefs and manifested a career he had never considered. And he found that this new career was indeed a dream opportunity that would not have become a reality had he stayed within the confines of what he believed he deserved.

When in doubt, always look to the emotion you desire – the feeling of happiness, success, joy, love, or contentment. Use pictures that remind you of that emotion. Broad illustrations allow you to expand your vibration and create opportunities that may be surprising!

Now you have a board that goes deeper than a vision board. It delves into the more important aspects of manifestation. It keeps you in that vessel of emotion, so you can be prepared to reach out for the opportunities that float by you on the river of life. It's up to you to decide!

Place your finished Emoti-Board where you can see it every day. Conscious viewing (and even touching) of the board creates more vibration, more energy that will propel your desires to you. And it will make you want to take action steps toward those dreams – to open those doors of opportunity and make solid choices to help you learn and grow.

PRACTICE

Create an Emoti-Board of your own using the directions above. You can do this in a group setting as well, inviting friends to bring magazines and other sources of pictures and words to share. The group setting invites a shared vibration, creating a powerful ripple effect into The Knowing. Put your Emoti-Board in a location where you can see it on a daily basis. Take a moment each day to look at your core word of emotion, and smile as you view the illustrations of that emotion.

SUMMARY

- You can create a visual representation of your purpose that will go deeper than vision boards.
- The Emoti-Board represents the emotion we truly desire to experience.
- Emoti-Boards (and vision boards) are extensions and forms of thought. We think about what we desire and expand on that thought by making statements, searching for appropriate pictures to illustrate the thought, and focusing on the creation of the board itself.
- Close your eyes and imagine yourself in the world you plan to create. Think about the feeling you will have when you have successfully manifested your dreams.
- Now search for ways to illustrate that feeling, and attach it to your board with the printed word.
- Divide your board into five primary groups: health, abundance, career or livelihood, relationships, and appearances. Illustrate each section.

CHAPTER 11: THE KEY OF THINKING IS THANKING

In an earlier chapter, I mentioned the old mantra, "Use it up, wear it out, make it do, or do without." I suggested that the first three parts of that mantra could be performed as grateful acts, instead of looking at frugality as "lack."

Be mindful of the way you look at frugality. Instead of considering it as a way to "get by," to make ends meet at the end of the month, or to survive in a less-than-perfect situation, reframe the idea. When you use something to its full potential, without waste or arrogance, you are honoring the fact that you have that item. For instance, many cooks insist on using every bit of the fish in their cooking, to show gratitude for the fish itself. Well-made shoes can be repaired by adding fresh soles, or you can mend tears in the seam of a coat. When you make do with an item that has lost its luster, but is still useable, you show gratitude for the maker and the planet we live on.

● ● ●

When you are grateful for something you have, and you take care of it, you create a ripple, a vibration of love. Gratitude is a vital part of creating. It is part of the vessel you climb into at the beginning of your journey of being alive. By thanking, you are thinking. By offering gratitude to something you may not yet have, you encourage it and welcome it into your reality.

Being grateful also allows you to see the optimistic side of a situation instead of focusing on the not-so-great stuff. If you make a decision to be grateful for everything that happens to you or around you, you not only become more optimistic, but you also draw in positive energy.

Showing gratitude allows your mind to accept that life is good. And that can boost your mood. Beware though, of falling into a rote "yeah, thanks" attitude and of expecting that your life will change overnight. You have to put some real thought into it.

• • •

Notice certain things that you are grateful for or can be grateful for. Find specifics – instead of just saying, "I'm grateful for my parents," say "I am grateful that Dad is willing to drive me to school in the morning."

You can show gratitude by listening to the happy call of the cardinal in the back yard or rain after a drought. I say "thank you" to the earth every time I eat or when I find a crisp apple in the CSA box.

Say thank you for solutions – or say thank you to someone you feel you need to make amends with. Pick up the phone and call a colleague, a relative, a friend, or a person with whom you have a strained relationship – and offer a heartfelt statement of thanks.

●　●　●

There should be no expectation of immediate reciprocity. Gratitude is something you give – and receive – with love. That love can only vibrate outward in some way, and you may or may not observe how it does that. You are only in control of your ability to offer thanks.

Gratitude can be spontaneous or more scheduled – such as writing in a gratitude journal every day. If you find writing your thanks in a journal each

morning for five minutes while you finish your morning coffee helps you balance the rest of the day,
then by all means do that. But I would suggest also
looking for opportunities to say thank you in other ways every day. Thank the person who delivers
your inter-office mail to your desk, the cashier in the
lunchroom, or the crossing guard who helps your
child cross the street every morning and afternoon.

When you think of gratitude, it creates a vision in
your mind. It offers an energetic spurt of energy – a
burst of emotion – sending a message to our brains
and outside our minds and bodies to The Knowing,
that this in fact is something that rides on love.

Love is The Knowing's favorite vibration, so
it immediately sets other vibrations in motion to
match yours (and others who are vibrating in the
same way). More good stuff starts heading your way
– even though you haven't even received anything
yet, you have offered the vibration of receiving and
The Knowing moves to match it. You give thanks
and then you receive.

●   ●   ●

How often can you do this? Over and over and

over. My parents were big on thank-you cards. They thanked everyone. They wrote cards to the mailman, the milkman, the guy who sold eggs to us, and the man at the gas station. Mom had us sit at the kitchen table and write thank-you cards to people who gave us gifts for our birthdays or to the moms who brought cupcakes for everyone in our class. They knew how important showing gratitude was.

Give thanks to someone today. Choose someone you may not see every day. Or find someone you see regularly and don't normally think about expressing your gratitude to. How about the doorman or the school bus driver or the guy you buy the hot dog from at the corner? You don't have to buy something to say thank you – just stop and say how much you appreciate their presence in your life.

Reach out to someone you haven't seen or heard from for a long time and ask how they are, and thank them for being a mentor or a friend or an example for others. Your kids? Kiss the baby and thank him for becoming a human being and landing his soul in that little body. Tell your high-school aged daughter how grateful you are that you can depend on her to do her best every day. Kids want and de-

serve thanks – they make our lives meaningful
and joyful.

●   ●   ●

Gratitude for the things you already have is the
first step toward change. Be thankful that there is a
service that results from that bill, a paycheck at the
end of the week, those fantastic little persons who
rock your everyday world with love.

I always think about "The Dick Van Dyke Show"
episodes, where Rob Petrie's son Richie runs up to
him after he comes home from work. Richie says,
"Daddy! What did you bring me?" Rob would hand
him the simplest thing, like a paper clip or a stick
of gum, and he would say enthusiastically "Thanks,
Daddy!" and run off set. Sure, it came off as a little
dopey, even then. But Richie gave us a little lesson
in being grateful for everything, and the gifting was
simply an excuse to have a moment of connection
with his dad. You could start to use this as a game
for your own family, by finding some random object
to give to the person who asks, "What did you bring
me?" Play this game with each other, yelling "Yay!"
whenever you're given a pen or empty candy bar
wrapper or a set of house keys.

Every connection, no matter how small, can be a reason for gratitude. You know that person on the phone who is dealing with your canceled credit card or the overcharge at the bank? You may not feel so grateful during the exchange. That is the very reason you want to find some gratitude. Changing your feeling of frustration to one of gratitude can change the entire dynamic of the phone call. That person may be handling much more than just your problem. A kind word stating that you know it is not his fault any of this happened and that you are grateful for his help, can bring down the heat and make him feel more valued.

● ● ●

Consider those tough circumstances. I had a very difficult first marriage. After I ended it and moved on with my life goals, I took some time to reflect on the marriage and the person I was married to. I realized how the relationship had changed my thought process and shown me my own depth of strength and optimism. Reaching out to him directly would not have been a smart idea, so I thanked him in my mind for being a part of my life and for giving me gifts of enlightenment along the way. His journey and his choices were very different from mine.

At the end of a second marriage, I understood more about the power of gratitude. When we separated, I was able to thank him directly for the contribution he made to my life.

He didn't understand what I was doing and had no idea how to react. He even seemed a little suspicious, perhaps thinking that I was secretly trying to trick him. But that didn't matter.

The thanking was for me. I needed to show him gratitude so I could release any binding thoughts that might hold me back from success. I have had moments of ungratefulness in the years since – but each time I was able to quickly flip that record over and play another song.

Even terrible circumstances – which I call "crappenings" - play good parts in your lives, by allowing you to discover your own infinite possibility, your strength, your power to change, and the incredible gift of being a human being who has free will and choice. Remember, that person may not see things in the same way. It is not your business or place to try to convince them, and it certainly does not mean that person should continue to be in your energetic field. You can still say goodbye with thanks; you can set yourself free with gratitude, and you can let go with love.

● ● ●

Your reality can change right now, given your thoughts. What you are experiencing in the now is from previous thoughts and actions. How do you want to live your life from now on? The first step is to change the way you are thinking, to create a vision of a new purpose, believe you are able to do so, and take small action steps in the direction of the goal. When you have an inspired thought, you have to trust it and act on it. If you focus on lack, you receive lack.

You do not need to know how it will happen, you just need to believe that it will.

Let's imagine you have to visit a food bank to stretch your budget this month. Instead of saying to yourself, "I am so ashamed! I can't even afford to put a decent meal on the table," take a breath and rearrange your emotions. Find that happiness canoe, and climb in. Say, "I am so grateful to have the food bank available to me this month!" If you have a bill you need to pay, say, "I am so grateful for (heat, water, car, etc), and that I have the money available to pay the bill!"

Why is gratitude such an important part of receiving? The upside down of this is that you must be grateful for things you have not yet received as well as those you have received. To do so creates a thought, a belief, that you have already received the emotional response to receiving. That not only changes your thought processes and the chemical response in your brain, but also changes the vibrational energy around you. The vibration that is sent to The Knowing attracts like vibrations and allows like situations to occur, giving you more to be thankful for.

PRACTICE

Make a list of the people you see every day, and choose one or two to personally thank. Pick out an appropriate thank-you card (or other form of communication), and write some heartfelt words about how they impact your life.

Think of one person in your past that may have

challenged you in some way. Think about the ways that person played a part in creating a positive aspect of yourself today. Thank that person in your mind – letting go of the anger or hurt – and focus on the way you have been successful in your life as a result.

SUMMARY

- Express gratitude by practicing reuse and recycle. "Use it up, wear it out, make it do" are all physical expressions of gratitude.
- Show gratitude for even the smallest of daily delights.
- Say thank you without expecting reciprocity.
- Make gratitude a game, find ways that you and others can receive and say "Thank you!"
- Be grateful for "crappenings" because they have helped you grow or learn in some way.
- Be grateful for solutions to a problem.
- Feel gratitude for things that haven't yet appeared!

CHAPTER 12: GIVING IS LIVING

On the other side of thanking is giving.

If you are the recipient of a gift, you feel gratitude and that feeling can alter your thought process and allow more to come to you through the attraction of like energy. It also causes the idea of generosity to ripple out from you.

A study published in the *Proceedings of the National Academy of Science* shows that when one person behaves generously, it inspires observers to behave generously later. The researchers found that altruism could spread from person to person to person to person. "As a result," they write, "each person in a network can influence dozens or even hundreds of people, some of whom he or she does not know and has not met."

But if you are on the giving end, you can benefit, too. Giving can cause the release of the feel-good hormone oxytocin for both the giver and the recipient, and create an oxytocin high that could spread to others in an ever-widening circle. It becomes contagious, like yawning. And giving to others even makes you want to increase your exercise and feel better about your lives.

The bottom line is you are more than yourself. You need the connectedness and the experience with others to complete the circle of energy.

*   *   *

There is a phenomenon in the ocean, where smaller lakes form from heavier water at the sea floor. It sounds crazy, right? Somehow, the salinity of areas of water increases three to eight times more than the surrounding water in the ocean. The brine-filled water is heavier than the ocean water, so it sinks to the bottom and forms lakes or pools of heavily salted water. The brine contains gases and minerals that provides energy to certain crea-tures that live near the lakes or pools. They are little worlds within a world.

The Knowing is like that great ocean. In taking on material (stardust) and salt and other things, you create your own reality within The Knowing, draw-ing in some communities and excluding others. You are a lake in an ocean.

The lake wouldn't exist without the ocean that surrounds it or the many sea creatures that have called it home. There is an ocean in every drop of water, as the old adage goes. By reaching out and offering something to someone else, you offer it to yourself. You are the same energy and stardust – just alive in a different form.

● ● ●

But how can you give when you have so little, you ask? Giving is not necessarily donating in the form of money, although that is one way you could do it. Money is energy in form, just like us, and it is a socially agreed-upon exchange of energy. Energy craves movement. Perhaps you can offer time to someone or to an organization. Or you could pick up trash, walk shelter dogs, or glean a field for those who lack food sources.

It can be even simpler in its form, but no less powerful. Have you ever given a compliment to someone or offered a genuine smile to someone who might rarely be noticed by others? Fred Rogers of *Mr. Rogers' Neighborhood* said to his viewers, "I like you just the way you are." He gave so much to countless children, just by looking into the camera and saying those simple words.

* * *

Your thoughts and gestures of giving should be mindful as well. When you simply react to the things that surround you, you move through the day without purposeful thought. You respond to that reckless driver that cut you off. You complain about the bills, your income, your kids, the coach of your favorite baseball team, the government, and on and on. That negative vibration ripples out to find like vibrations – and negative energy comes back.

As a result you stay locked in that negative space. You recreate situations over and over again until they become so comfortable you no longer notice. It has become your normal.

The first step is to do what we discussed in the previous chapter – offer thanks to the events of the past, and make steps to show gratitude to others.

The next step is to give back.

* * *

Create a vibration of love and kindness by giving a donation to a local youth league. Volunteer an afternoon to a political candidate who aligns his beliefs with yours. Drop some change in that charity's donation jar. Do whatever you can that feels good and right and shakes out the dust of the old negativity.

I don't believe you have to buy into the rigid principle of tithing or giving away 10% of your money. That is confining and creates a feeling of obligation and resentment. Sometimes you give less or more. Or sometimes you can give in ways other than money. And although I would strongly recommend that you should have no expectations when you offer these gifts, The Knowing always seems to reciprocate in kind. No matter how small the offering, the resulting energy will blow the doors of opportunity off their hinges. The belief that you are successful allows the mindset of philanthropy. The more you give, the more you receive.

An acquaintance once told me, "Where I'm from [India], guests are God. We will feed them well, even if we have nothing for ourselves. It is joy to serve another."

It is a joy to serve another.

* * *

How wonderful would it be to treat every stranger as if you and he were God or The Knowing, or whatever you choose to call that infinite and aware consciousness? How would your business change if you treated your employees and customers as if they were the most important person in the room?

Fyodor Dostoevsky wrote in his journal, "And it is so simple... The one thing is — love thy neighbor as thyself — that is the one thing. That is all, nothing else is needed. You will instantly find how to live. Though it is an old truth, repeated and read ten million times, yet, it is discovered. The knowledge of life is higher than life, the knowledge of the laws of happiness is higher than happiness...If only everyone wanted it, then everything would be right in an instant."

The Knowing is more than just your own life. It transcends petty argument and violent hate. It is love or lack of love that guides you and others through that journey of being alive. In giving, you rise above the fray - and you discover how to be alive.

Understand that old feelings will bubble to the surface now and again. That's perfectly normal. You may have lived in a box of drama for so long that you have learned to survive on it. It is your bread and butter. But if you remain aware and purposeful in your thoughts, it gets easier – and better. By helping others achieve their dreams, you are helping yourself – the lake in an ocean concept. And you will begin to create the stuff of your dreams.

You can change your reality by using purposeful thought and directing your positive energy to others. You release the cycle of negative vibrations around you that have brought similar energy to you. Through positive giving, you receive positive energy.

PRACTICE

Today, treat every person you meet as if they are The Knowing. Imagine that each person is there to change your life. Give your full attention to him or her and listen carefully to their needs or desires. If you can help, do so. If you can't, then offer support and encouragement – this is also a form of giving.

SUMMARY

- Giving to someone can alter his or her thought process and allow more to come to them through the attraction of like energy.
- Giving can cause the release of the feel-good hormone oxytocin for both the giver and the recipient.
- We need the connectedness, the experience with others to complete the circle of energy.
- By reaching out and offering something to someone else, we offer it to ourselves because we are the same energy and stardust – just *alive* in a different form.
- When you simply react to the things that surround you, you move through the day without purposeful thought.
- Gratitude for the things you already have is the first step toward change. The next step is to give back.

CHAPTER 13: TAKING ACTION

Now that you have had some practice recognizing your true goals, you are ready to accept one more step in purposeful thinking and being alive.

You must take action.

You are made of stardust and energy, remember? Stardust has to shine, and energy craves movement. So doing something – anything – can allow your amazing self to blast off into parts unknown. You have all that power collecting inside you, hanging out with the protons and electrons and thought soup, and it is anxiously waiting for ground control to give the thumbs-up for adventure. Taking action is the signal.

● ● ●

You now have the tools to create a life of your dreams. You have learned that thought doesn't only exist in your body's mind, but it also lives in The Knowing. You understand that some events and circumstances are a result of the thoughts of others. You have come to accept the idea that you are truly in control of your thoughts and that by changing your thoughts you can change your life. You express gratitude, and you give in so many delightful ways.

So now you have to paddle that canoe if you want to truly experience this life.

● ● ●

Small, seemingly insignificant actions can cause a ripple to occur in that river, and it will get bigger and ripple farther out all the way to the ocean and eventually cause a wave. Make sure your nose is pointed toward your dream, not back at your past or in the direction of any obstacles.

Pay attention to your statements, your moods, your responses. Act as if you are already the person you want to be, in the position in which you desire. Feel the success and exhilaration, the contentment and happiness.

If you strive to reach business success, read related books. Take workshops, find courses online or at colleges. Talk to people who are in a level of expertise that you want to reach. Leave behind the old beliefs that you cannot reach any higher. Learning is growing.

If you are surrounded by those who hold you back, ground you to your present station, or otherwise cause you to lose faith in your abilities, stand up for yourself and insist on their support. Some will not know how to be comfortable with you once you have started to move forward. They will make comments that might latch on to those old feelings of inadequacy or low self-esteem, or even guilt. This can be the most difficult hurdle of all. You may have to walk away from certain relationships in order to keep taking action in the direction of your new dreams. Whatever happens, express gratitude that those relationships helped you discover yourself. Intend that your success will inspire others to find their own truth and to flip their own records to the positive music they would rather hear.

●   ●   ●

Each person around you has set out on a journey on his or her own. No matter how difficult, how despicable these people seem, they are navigating the river with an original goal that may or may not have changed along the way. But what remains right now is the opportunity.

You have the opportunity to look at the relationship, despite the circumstances, say thank you for allowing the chance to learn and grow, and move forward to be the best you.

I must admit to you that I have moments when I forget about all of this. I forget that I am alive, and I allow mundane arguments, misunderstandings, and world events get to my core. I find that my face gets tight, my brow furrows, and I worry how I am going to accomplish certain things. Sometimes I feel uninspired or hurried by the clock. Even someone skilled in being alive must practice purposeful thought from moment to moment, to remember to use FEAR and continue to navigate the river without pushing it. I can honestly say that I shake off these feelings pretty quickly, jump back in the canoe, and continue my incredible ride.

● ● ●

The art of being being alive means that you find love in all efforts. Allowing yourself to remain stuck, to live in a rut, is not loving to yourself or to the others – even the ones who try to hold you back or who direct negative comments to you. Pull yourself out of the mud first, then reach out to offer a hand to those who are still in it. Make sure you stand strong enough to help them out and not allow yourself to be pulled back in. You are not alone in this adventure, and just as others will appear in response to your newfound purpose, you will also be a part of someone else's manifestation to offer guidance or inspiration.

Several years ago, my then-boyfriend and I were driving in Florida when the air conditioning failed in our rental car. The rental company promised they would dispatch a driver with a replacement car, and we headed to a local diner to wait. After we ordered our meal, we saw a young woman come in with two young children in tow. She leaned down next to the older child and whispered, "Only a drink, sweetie, I don't have any more money." The little boy solemnly looked up at her and nodded.

It was nearly midnight, and I saw the exhaustion in her eyes and the eyes of the two children. I remembered a time long ago when I spent hours in a late-night diner, waiting with my own children for the safety of a sunrise. In an instant, I understood her, and her predicament did not need to be explained or analyzed. She simply needed to know someone cared.

I motioned to our server, and when she came over, I asked her to allow the woman and her children to order from the menu. We would cover the bill. "Don't tell her who is paying for it," I asked. The server looked at the woman for a moment, and when she looked back at me, her tear-filled eyes told me everything. She nodded and went to the kitchen. After a few moments, she returned and approached the family's table. "Ma'am, it's your lucky night!" She smiled at the woman. "You are the one hundredth person to come in today. Your meal is on us!"

The young mother's face transformed. Her face relaxed around her eyes and mouth. She looked at the server first in disbelief, then in relief. The two children watched their mother's face, and they reacted in kind, smiling at first the mother and then the server. The youngest child hopped in place, even though he wasn't sure what was happening. He just knew that in the grand scheme of things, today was wonderful.

As the family ate hamburgers and fries, the young woman hugged her children and brightly told

them, "See? We're going to be okay! Jesus loves us!"
It didn't matter if Jesus was the focus of the young
mother's gratitude. It didn't matter whether she
had a different view of faith than myself or perhaps
that of the server. Her belief in the existence of a
father-god presented itself in a loving energy that
matched my own awareness of The Knowing. A simple action started a chain reaction. The smiles were
solid evidence – from the teary-eyed server, to the
cook who looked out at us and gave us the thumbs-
up, to our own smiles, knowing that the ripple was
real, and it would continue in so many directions
and in so many ways. Our replacement vehicle arrived, and we went on our way.

• • •

Taking action in the direction of your dreams is
an important step to achievement. This does not
mean that you are alone in this adventure. You are
here with others who are all part of The Knowing.
You have a chance to explore and play and expand
your awareness, so that you can share it with others
when you again become immersed in The Knowing.

While you're here, at times you'll knock into each
other's manifestations like bumper cars or merge

into them like clouds of cream into coffee. Each event, each meeting, each and every person who is in the middle of being alive, will change us in some way. You are unlimited in your reach, eternal in your spirit, and you can play this ever-expanding game to the best of your ability.

Do something – anything – that makes you learn or grow. Make someone else smile or feel better about themselves, without expecting any thanks or reciprocation. Pick up the paddles, and dig into the fluid motion of the river in the direction of your dreams. Small actions will take off and shine on their own, and you won't have to look. Once you have incorporated this type of action in each and every day, the result is like watching a sky full of fireworks. You can't follow each trail of light, you just know that all of it is beautiful.

PRACTICE

Write down your purpose or goal at the top of a blank sheet of paper. Now list some small action steps you can take in the direction of this dream. Write all of them down, no matter how small you think they are. Taking 5 minutes per day to focus on your dream, reading a book that relates to your goal, calling a mentor to discuss your plans, or whatever works for you. These all help set the proper vibration in motion.

To change your surroundings, take action in small ways. Sweep the kitchen floor or straighten the clutter on the coffee table. Drop some change in a busker's hat. Compliment a stranger on his smile. Buy a meal for someone in secret.

SUMMARY

- You must take action.
- You are truly in control of your thoughts and by changing them, you can change your life.
- You have to paddle that canoe if you want to truly experience this life.
- Small, seemingly insignificant actions can cause a ripple to occur, which can eventually cause a wave of change.
- Act as if you are already the person you want to be, in the position in which you desire. Feel the emotion.
- You may have to let go of some relationships that keep you from progressing. Say thank you for having the chance to learn and grow, and move forward to be the best you.

CONCLUSION

Now you are at the end of this book, and at the beginning of a new awareness. You are beginning to understand how you can play with unlimited possibility, even in your limited form. You might even find that you have fleeting memories of how it once was, as part of The Knowing, bending reality and expanding consciousness. Just by reading this book, you have opened your mind up to possibility. But you didn't have to become aware to manifest your thoughts - you have been doing it all along. You have been creating a life based on your thoughts, your emotions and your desires. And you can change everything right now.

Embrace the fact that you have the power to choose your future path. You chose to become you through thought. By choosing your thoughts wisely, you can choose your future. Make decisions based on how you want to feel and what would best achieve your desired outcome. Change your fear to FEAR. Strengthen your ability to manifest your dreams by using the exercises in each chapter, and create an Emoti-Board that captures the essence of the new you.

You are alive, on a continuous occurrence of birth and death, and you are connected to everything around you. Dreaming, imagining, and feeling the emotional high of a wonderful future is the spark that ignites the flame of reality. Whatever you truly desire is only a thought away.

Practice the art of being alive, and master the thought of you!

Made in the USA
Lexington, KY
22 November 2019